KEY TO
MURDER

A Play

STEWART BURKE

To Margaret

With every good wish

Stewart Burke

1995

SAMUEL · FRENCH

FRENCH

LONDON

NEW YORK TORONTO SYDNEY HOLLYWOOD

KEY TO MURDER

First presented by the Repertory Players at the Comedy Theatre, London, with the following cast of characters:

Mrs Dacre	Varley Thomas
Robert Mallin	Alexander John
Maggy Fairchild	Beryl Baxter
Peter Clinton	Geoffrey Colville
Eva Mallin	Joan Peart
George Lawrence	Peter Noel Cook
Ed Ryde	Robert Ayres

The play directed by Anthony Marlowe

The action takes place in Maggy Fairchild's London flat

ACT I   Thursday afternoon
(the CURTAIN is lowered during this act to denote the passing of the hours until midnight)

ACT II
  SCENE 1   Friday morning
  SCENE 2   Friday night
  SCENE 3   Saturday morning

ACT III
  SCENE 1   Saturday evening
  SCENE 2   Later the same night

Time—the present

Please note our NEW ADDRESS:

Samuel French Ltd
52 Fitzroy Street London W1P 6JR
Tel: 01 - 387 9373

ACT I

Maggy Fairchild's flat in London. Thursday afternoon, five o'clock

The set comprises the bedroom and the lounge, the latter taking up the larger part of the stage

From the rear wall of the lounge an archway leads to the hall, in which is a narrow table with a bowl of flowers. This archway is curtained. A door leads off the lounge to the kitchen. In the fireplace, which is flanked by low shelf fitments containing books, ornaments, vases of flowers, is an electric fire. To one side of the archway is a barred window, framed by velvet curtains, to the other a wine cabinet, well stocked. Furniture consists of a settee, a basket chair and a modern swivel rocker. A telephone is on a small writing-bureau. Wall lamps flank the archway and fireplace, which has a Degas or similar print over it. On the mantelpiece are matches, a box of menthol cigarettes, and a gold cigarette-lighter. In the bureau is a drawer containing letters, and on top a writing-pad, Biro, desk lamp, and copy of the "Stage". A coffee-table stands below the window when not in use

In the bedroom a single divan bed with low headboard is set against the dividing wall, forming a barrier between the two rooms. A door leads from the lounge. There is a barred window, and under it a dressing-table holding cosmetics, jewel-box, brushes, a lamp, and a copy of "Spotlight". Letters are loose in a drawer. A high wardrobe contains Maggy's clothes, amongst which is a white négligé. A stool faces the dressing-table, and there is also a basket chair. (See plan of set, page 52)

As the CURTAIN *rises, the telephone is ringing. A vacuum-cleaner stands by the lounge window*

Mrs Dacre, the daily help, in a nylon overall, enters from the kitchen, goes to the bureau, and lifts the receiver

Mrs Dacre (*on the telephone*) Hallo.... No, Miss Fairchild is out at rehearsal. ... Who? ... No, he's not here. ... Yes, I'll ask him to ring you when he arrives. Who shall I say called? ... Right, I won't forget, Mrs Mallin. Good-bye.

She is on her way back to kitchen when the doorbell rings

Mrs Dacre goes out through the archway. There is a murmur of voices off, then she returns with Robert Mallin, a quiet, good-looking man in his thirties, wearing horn-rims which he occasionally removes to gesture with. He carries a briefcase containing a T.V. script

Mrs Dacre She said she'd be home around five o'clock, sir.

Robert (*glancing at his watch*) It's coming up to that now.

Mrs Dacre Then she'll be here any moment, I expect. She's rehearsing for a new T.V. series, she told me.

Robert moves to the swivel rocker and puts his briefcase on it

Robert I haven't seen you here before.

Mrs Dacre Well, I only started this morning. I like working for a lady who's out all day. Then we don't get under each other's feet.

Robert goes to the wine cabinet and is considering what to have when Mrs Dacre goes up to him

That's right, sir, make yourself at home. Only we're a bit low on the gin.

He gives her a significant look. She reacts with a touch of embarrassed guilt, then goes to the window and is about to draw the curtains when she glances down into the street

Mrs Dacre Is that your car down there?

Robert (*pouring a Scotch*) M'm?

Mrs Dacre Parked outside. Is it yours—the Silver Rolls?

Robert Yes. (*He takes his drink to the rocker, sits, places the glass on the small table, opens his briefcase and takes out a T.V. script, which he starts to work on, making changes with a Biro*)

Mrs Dacre Very swish (*She draws the curtains*) Mind, you're not supposed to park in this road. We're a no-parking zone (*She unplugs the vacuum-cleaner*) Even people who live here aren't allowed to park outside. Miss Fairchild keeps her Mini round the back.

Robert I know. But my car won't go through the gateway.

Mrs Dacre pushes the vacuum-cleaner down level with Robert as she chats on, and begins coiling the flex

Mrs Dacre Still, not to worry. I shouldn't think they'd give you a parking ticket, not as it's a Rolls. The traffic wardens will think you're an oil shriek.

Robert sighs, swinging his chair away from her and trying to continue with his work. She pushes the vacuum-cleaner into kitchen, returning a few seconds later with a duster, which she flicks over the mantelpiece, wine cabinet, bureau and telephone, moving around

Mrs Dacre This place is condemned, you know. Every house has to come down. Most of the tenants have gone already. Can't blame 'em really. Must be a bit creepy here at night, wouldn't fancy it myself. I don't live in, you know. There's no-one underneath now. That flat's been empty for ages, so Miss Fairchild told me. (*She moves down beside Robert to dust the small table, holding his drink*) You'd think she'd live in a modern block, wouldn't you, her being famous and everything. One of them upside down dominoes with all mod cons . . . Know her well, do you?

Robert removes his horn-rims and looks up at her with a patient smile

Robert Don't let me keep you from your work, Mrs—er . . .

Mrs Dacre Mrs Dacre. There, I let you in and forgot to ask your name. Are you a personal friend of Miss Fairchild?

Robert I'm writing the scripts for the new T.V. series she's going to star in.

Mrs Dacre Are you a famous author, then?

Robert is once more working on his script. Mrs Dacre moves to the window and glances out

Well, you must be—a Rolls Royce and all. (*She looks at him*) And you didn't get that with Green Shield stamps.

Robert wearily looks ceilingwards as she comes down to plague him again

Robert Actually, my name's Robert Mallin, but I don't suppose you've ever heard of me.

Mrs Dacre Yes, I have. There was a phone message for you. Your wife wants you to ring her.

Robert returns his script to his briefcase, rises and goes to the telephone. Mrs Dacre watches him curiously as he dials. He gives her a look

Mrs Dacre scuttles into the kitchen

Robert (*on the telephone*) Eva? . . . Hallo, darling. I've only just arrived at Maggy's flat. . . . Well, it was very late when we finished bridge, so I stayed the night at my club. . . . I did phone you this morning but you were out. . . . I'm sorry, I forgot you'd invited people to lunch. (*He is plainly suffering as he is nagged from the other end*) I said I'm sorry, Eva, but I must be free of social commitments when I'm trying to write these scripts. . . . Very well, take a taxi and call for me here.

The front door is heard to open and slam

Maggy Fairchild appears in the hall. She pauses to leave her handbag on the hall table and glances towards Robert, who is still on the telephone. At twenty-seven she is beautiful and dresses with the flair of a star. She moves down to the hearthrug

Robert sees her and gives her a wave of greeting

(*On the telephone*) Yes, Eva, all right. In about fifteen minutes. Good-bye, darling.

He replaces the receiver and goes to Maggy, taking both her hands in his and smiling. She smiles back

Hallo, Maggy.

Maggy (*teasingly*) You fraud, Robert, you didn't show up for the read-through. Why?

Robert The author has to accord you the usual privileges.

He helps to remove Maggy's coat

Maggy We didn't tear the script to ribbons, if that's what you mean. In fact, I thought it was marvellous.

Robert You're being kind.

Maggy No, honestly, I think it's a winner. Brilliant. And my part—(*she clasps her hands together enthusiastically*)—it's a dream. Just the sort of role I love playing. Full of life and vitality and sparkle.

Robert I wrote it with you in mind, Maggy.

Maggy You're a darling, Robert. (*She kisses him lightly*) Don't tell your wife I did that.

Robert I never tell Eva anything, it isn't good for her to know.

Maggy Does she get jealous?

Robert I'm careful not to give her cause.

Maggy (*teasingly*) Meaning you're—discreet?

Robert Could be. Well, now, how did the rehearsal go?

Maggy Oh, we only walked through our parts after the read-through. You see, we hadn't a full cast. No leading man.

Robert Pity about that.

Maggy Did you know Alec had backed out?

Robert Yes, Peter told me Alec had a film offer.

Maggy Flew off to Hollywood at a moment's notice.

Robert He had no definite contract with us, so we couldn't hold him.

Maggy But who are we going to put in his place? Peter seemed rather vague about it. He said we could decide when he got here today.

Robert What time is he coming?

Maggy He'll be here at any moment. He was driving behind me but he couldn't get his Mercedes through my gateway. I can only just squeeze my Mini in. Now he's gone off in search of a meter. He's had too many parking-tickets to risk leaving his car in the road. But *you* don't seem to mind. That's the beauty of owning a Rolls.

Robert I'll move it later, if you think I should.

Maggy Oh, we don't get many traffic wardens round here.

Mrs Dacre enters from the kitchen

Mrs Dacre Oh, hallo, Miss Fairchild. I didn't hear you come in.

Maggy (*smiling*) Hallo, Mrs Dacre.

Mrs Dacre Like some tea, would you, madam?

Maggy That would be lovely. Everything been all right today?

Mrs Dacre Yes, I gave the flat a thorough going-over. I hope you noticed.

Maggy Oh, yes. Yes, I did. Were there any phone messages?

Mrs Dacre Only one for Mr Mallin.

Robert Eva wanted to remind me that we're going to a cocktail party. She's calling here soon.

Maggy Then we'll wait tea until she comes.

Mrs Dacre Very well, madam.

Mrs Dacre returns to the kitchen

Maggy Help yourself to a drink, Robert, while I freshen up.

Maggy takes her coat into the bedroom, switching on the lights, closing the door behind her. She hangs the coat in the wardrobe, then goes to the dressing-table to sit down and tidy her hair. The doorbell rings, Robert moves up to the arch

Mrs Dacre comes to the kitchen doorway

Robert I'll answer it.

Mrs Dacre returns to the kitchen, Robert goes into the hall and returns with Peter Clinton, a mature T.V. producer, pleasant and good-tempered

Peter Maggy here yet?

Robert (*moving to the wine cabinet*) In the bedroom. (*He indicates a drink*)

Peter Make it a neat Scotch, please.

Robert (*pouring the drink*) I haven't told her yet.

Peter Coward.

Robert I thought you'd prefer to do so yourself.

Peter In that case make it a double.

Robert Why all the fuss? Maggy may welcome the idea of George Lawrence as her leading man.

Peter You have to be joking.

Robert (*taking the drink to Peter*) They did a play together on Broadway.

Peter That's why. She thinks it was *his* fault *The Tiger* closed after only two weeks.

Robert Luck of the game.

Peter Maggy doesn't believe that. She's convinced George wrecked the whole show. When you suggested him for the part I had a strong suspicion Maggy would object.

Robert Correction. I didn't suggest George—my wife did. She has a thing about him.

Peter You don't mind?

Robert Eva suits herself. Anyway, we can't upset her, as she's writing the cheques for this pilot episode.

Peter Wish I could back it myself but my bank manager would throw a fit. He keeps reminding me about my overdraft, as it is.

Robert (*sitting on the settee*) You could sell that great Mercedes.

Peter Impossible. I haven't finished paying all the instalments. And I need it to keep up the old image. Leo likes to deal with people who look successful. And we want him to book this T.V. series, don't we? Must keep on the right side of dear old Leo.

Robert (*raising his glass*) Here's to Leo.

Peter Leo. And if he doesn't okay the pilot episode—may he rot in hell!

They drink to this

Robert Think we'll get a long series?

Peter I'm hoping for a twenty-six-week contract, with options to continue indefinitely. You've written a damned good script, Robert.

Maggy enters from the bedroom, carrying the copy of "Spotlight"

Maggy Hallo, so you found a meter?

Peter Yes, after cruising round for a while. Want a drink, Maggy?

Maggy Not just now, we'll be having tea presently.

Robert (*rising*) Oh, do have a sherry or something—just to buck you up.

Maggy Why should I need bucking up?

Robert Well, I thought—it's all right, nothing.

Maggy (*looking from one to the other*) You're both looking rather odd. What have you been saying while I was in the bedroom?

Peter Just—er—discussing a possible leading man for you, Maggy.

Maggy Good. (*She sits on settee and opens "Spotlight"*) Well, make yourselves comfortable and I'll go through *Spotlight* and see if I can find a suitable actor.

Robert hovers beind the settee. Peter sits in the rocker, looking far from "comfortable"

Robert I don't think you need *Spotlight*. You see, Peter already has someone in mind.

Maggy Really? That's fine. Who, Peter?

Peter (*looking out front*) George Lawrence.

"Spotlight" slips from Maggy's fingers to the floor. She looks tense

Maggy You're joking.

Robert No, he's quite serious.

Maggy George, of all people! Oh, no, no!

Peter George has a "name", a public, Maggy. He's a good actor.

Robert Very good.

Maggy Robert, you can't really mean that. You saw him in *The Tiger* on Broadway. Don't you remember what a dreadful performance he gave—not only on the opening night but time after time—until the show had to close.

Peter (*rising*) Look, Maggy, he wasn't well, he told me so.

Maggy He'd been drinking and taking drugs. (*rising and moving away*) I'm sorry, if you must have George, then count me out.

Peter Be reasonable, Maggy. George needs a chance to prove himself. He hasn't worked since that Broadway flop.

Maggy (*swinging round*) I haven't worked, either—since that Broadway flop!

Robert But George needs to re-establish himself . . .

Maggy So does Peter, so do I. And you, too, Robert. This is your great opportunity to make a name for yourself—as a T.V. scriptwriter. Are you going to risk letting George shatter all our chances?

Peter He's not as bad as all that. You're usually so kind and sympathetic towards struggling actors and actresses.

Maggy George isn't a struggling actor—he's a man who had a fine reputation once. Then he threw it all away, took to drink and drugs and behaved as if he just didn't care any more. I feel sorry for him, yes, but will Leo be as tolerant as you and Robert are? Leo never feels sorry for anyone.

Robert We all know he's a hard nut.

Peter And a sanctimonious old humbug! Carries the plate round in chapel and everyone must be whiter-than-white.

Maggy Exactly. One hint of scandal about anyone and he won't have them on his payroll. If he heard about George . . .

Peter But George has taken a cure. He's been out of the drug cupboard for nine months. And he doesn't drink now. He told me so.

Maggy Well, he could easily revert to type under stress. And a long T.V. series does call for iron nerves. Look, it isn't only his drug-taking and compulsive drinking Leo could object to. There's something else.

Robert Well, what?

Maggy George is "gay".

Peter Rubbish.

Robert He's a womanizer.

Maggy That's his alibi.

Peter You've got it all wrong.

Maggy I haven't, Peter. George told me himself, during the run of the Broadway play. He came to my dressing-room one night after the show and just talked and talked . . .

Peter He was probably tanked up.

Maggy (*sitting on the settee*) *In vino veritas.*

Robert That tag doesn't always apply. (*He sits in the basket chair*)

Maggy In his case I think it did. He was very convincing. He even gave me the names of the men in his life.

Peter So what? Even if it's true it's no concern of ours.

Maggy I'm not setting myself up in judgement.

Robert No?

Maggy No, Robert. I'm merely trying to point out why we can't have George in the series.

Peter Just because he's a bit "camp"? In our permissive society anything goes and nobody cares a damn.

Maggy Leo does, you know he does. He goes in for good, clean, family entertainment. And he likes his actors to lead decent, normal lives with no dodgy shadows to spoil their publicity. Why, he won't even use actors and actresses who have been *divorced*!

Robert That narrows the field a bit.

Peter Leo needn't know about George. And if we turn him down now and he goes back to drugs I shall have that on my conscience.

Maggy And if he comes into the series and wrecks it? (*rising, to Peter*) Think of yourself, Peter. You need this T.V. chance and so do I. Neither of us has had much luck lately. Why should we take unnecessary risks, cripple ourselves for the sake of one unreliable actor?

Peter Robert doesn't have to write him up too big. You'll come in for the more starry part, Maggy.

Maggy There won't be a series to star in.

Robert I don't think a gloomy outlook is going to get us anywhere. I suggest we do as Peter says—give George Lawrence his chance, then if he doesn't measure up . . .

Maggy (*passionately*) Oh, for heaven's sake, what's the matter with you both? This series could mean a great deal to all three of us. Do we have to invite trouble? If we keep George we'll fail. We're bound to fail. George doesn't care about other people or what he does to them. In New York he blamed the producer, the other artists and eventually the backer for closing the show. It never occurred to him to blame *himself*!

Robert strolls round behind the settee. Pause

Robert It's personal, isn't it, Maggy?

Maggy What's that supposed to mean?

Robert The play folded on Broadway and you and Ed Ryde split. You feel if the show had continued your marriage might have held. . . .

Maggy My private life has nothing whatever to do with this. You were there, you saw the hash George made of things. The agony every other member of the cast went through when they had to play a scene with him on stage.

Peter George has changed since then.

Maggy Look, I sweated blood throughout the whole of that ghastly fortnight. And if you imagine I'm going through all that again, then I'm sorry to disappoint you. Keep George, if you must, but I don't need a clairvoyant to tell me your T.V. series, Robert, will die before it's born.

The doorbell rings

Robert That's probably Eva. We'll have to cut the discussion now. I doubt if my wife will be interested.

Robert goes out into hall

Maggy moves to Peter

Peter Don't mention anything about this in front of Eva Mallin. She likes George. Besides, she's putting up the money. We couldn't hope to launch this pilot without her backing.

Maggy I thought Robert was taking the risk.

Peter Robert carries no more than the loose change in his pocket. Eva Mallin is the daughter of Marcus Hemingway, the soap millionaire. Didn't you know?

Maggy shakes her head

Robert enters with Eva Mallin, a tall woman, sophisticated, with a jealous streak in her. She is expensively dressed in a couture cocktail gown and fur coat. She is speaking irritably as they enter

Eva And if you ever let me down again . . .

Robert All right, not now. (*Socially*) I think you know Maggy Fairchild— and Peter, of course.

Maggy Hallo, Mrs Mallin, how are you?

Eva Had a good day, all of you?

Peter It was only a read-through. We hope to get down to serious work next week.

Robert helps Eva to remove her coat. She leaves it with him, together with her handbag

Eva Good. And Robert's script—how was that?

Peter Fine.

Maggy Do sit down, Mrs Mallin. I'm sure you'd like some tea.

Maggy picks up "Spotlight" and notices Robert hovering with Eva's coat and handbag

Oh, put those things in my bedroom, Robert. (*She gives him "Spotlight"*)
Eva We mustn't be long. We're on our way to a cocktail party.
Robert (*at the bedroom door*) I'd like some tea, I missed lunch.
Eva Whose fault was that? It's an hour's run to Weybridge and you know how I hate being late for anything.

Robert takes her coat and bag into the bedroom and returns

Maggy goes into the kitchen

Peter An hour to Weybridge—in *that* car.
Eva (*sits on settee*) My father didn't buy us the Rolls to kill ourselves in. Has anyone a menthol cigarette?
Peter Yes, Maggy smokes them.

Peter takes the box from the mantelpiece and offers it to Eva. Robert gives her a light for the cigarette

Eva So everything went well today. No hitches of any kind?
Peter None that can't be ironed out—in time.
Eva Robert didn't choose to be there, I understand?
Robert They didn't need me. Besides, I had some work to catch up on, so I stayed at the club.
Eva It *is* possible to work at home.

Peter sits beside Eva on the settee

Peter I haven't had a chance to talk to you personally about all this, Eva. We do appreciate what you're doing to help. Naturally when Leo gives us the green light to go ahead and starts talking money and contracts, you'll be paid back every penny, with interest. You can have that in writing, if you like.
Eva And you're quite satisfied with your cast? I was wondering if there are any changes you might care to make. Last-minute second thoughts, for instance.
Peter Why do you ask, Eva?
Eva I've never been too happy about—Maggy Fairchild.
Peter She's a wonderful actress.
Eva Oh, I know she used to be very good. But I've read Robert's script and I visualized someone—younger.
Peter Maggy's only twenty-seven.
Eva Really? You surprise me!
Robert Leo likes Maggy.
Eva I'm sure all *men* like her.

Maggy looks round the kitchen door

Maggy Can anyone mend electric kettles? Mine is staging a sit-down strike and Mrs Dacre and I haven't a clue about electrical gadgets.

Eva It's no use asking Robert, Miss Fairchild. He's hopeless at anything practical.

Peter I'll have a look but I don't guarantee results.

Maggy Thanks, Peter, you're an angel.

Peter follows Maggy into kitchen

Eva rises and strolls round the room critically

Eva So this is where she lives. Rather a shabby street, isn't it? And that door downstairs is almost off its hinges. All the stray cats and dogs in the neighbourhood must wander into the hallway.

Robert The flat is pleasant enough.

Eva (*going to him*) And you know the flat well, of course.

Robert Indicating?

Eva That you've been here before.

Robert Of course I've been here before.

Eva Many times?

Robert No, not . . .

Eva Last night, for instance?

Robert (*startled*) Last night?

Eva I don't believe in private detectives. I find the service degrading, though I'm quite sure they could provide me with all the evidence I need.

Robert (*walking away from her*) Evidence for what?

Eva A divorce. Do you like the sound of that word—or does it send icy shivers down your spine? Just imagine, darling, being out in the cold again, having to rely on your writing efforts to make a living. What a shock that would be, after you've been kept in luxury all these years.

Robert Eva, why do you torture yourself? Maggy Fairchild—is that what you think?

Eva You didn't come home last night—and it wasn't the first time.

Robert Can you blame me? At least when I'm at the club I can call my soul my own.

Eva (*significantly*) I rang the club this morning.

Robert reacts. Then he begins to storm round the room

Robert I wonder you *don't* employ a private detective. But no—you wouldn't do that because it would spoil your fun. Better, far better to play the game all by yourself—snooping, spying, phoning round . . . Oh, how you revel in it. The joy of finding me out in a lie.

Eva Then you admit you lie?

Robert Of course I damn well lie! Any wife who behaves the way you do deserves lies!

Eva Where were you last night?

Robert Oh, find out! And have fun in the process.

Eva Don't push me too far, Robert. It's always struck me as strange that the wife is the last to know.

Robert To know what, for God's sake.

Eva (*going to him*) It *is* Maggy Fairchild, isn't it?

Robert turns his back on Eva

When she was mentioned for the series I should have guessed, shouldn't I? That hurried trip to America when she was opening in a new play . . .

Robert (*swinging round*) I went to see my publishers.

Eva (*laughing contemptuously*) Your publishers! That élite little magazine that pays you a handful of dollars for a story and assures you of its prestige value. Half-a-dozen acceptances from them wouldn't cover your air fare. So let's stop pretending, shall we?

Robert All right, I'm in love with Maggy. That's what you want to hear, isn't it?

Eva Is that the truth?

Robert It makes no difference whether it's the truth or not—it's what you want to hear.

Eva moves away from him, her expression bitter. She sits in the rocker. Robert comes and stands over her

You're one of those unfortunate women, Eva, who imagine that because they have money they can *buy* a man, then use him as a puppet, pull the strings this way and that, make him into a willing and adoring slave for life. No marriage can exist for long on that level, not for me, anyway. I trust you and I expect you to trust me. If you can't—or won't—then it's just too bad.

Eva I said I'd back this series as a last hope. I imagined you might appreciate all I'm trying to do for you.

Robert There are other ways of helping, you know, besides money. But that's your weapon, and my God, how you use it!

Eva (*sadly*) We can't all choose our weapons, Robert. What else do I have?

Maggy enters from the kitchen with a plate of cakes which she gives to Robert to hold while she fetches the coffee-table from under the window and puts it before the settee. Peter enters from the kitchen with a tray of tea things

Maggy Peter's a marvel. He found the fault in that kettle and fixed it right away.

Eva You need a man about the house, Miss Fairchild . . . permanently.

Maggy reacts with some surprise to the barbed remark. She sits on the settee to pour out tea

Maggy How do you like your tea, Mrs Mallin?

Eva Strong, please. No milk or sugar.

Robert These cakes look good.

Maggy Do help yourself.

Robert offers the plate to Eva, then Peter, who both decline, then he takes one himself, replacing the plate on the table

Robert I missed lunch today.

Eva My husband misses a lot of things—he works so hard. That's the worst of being a successful author.

Her sarcasm is not lost on the others, who look embarrassed by it. Peter takes a cup of tea to Eva, then collects his own cup and sits on the settee beside Maggy

Peter I think it was a good idea, keeping the cast small to begin with. If the weather doesn't hold, though, we're going to find it dicey getting the location scenes shot. I suppose there's no alternative, Rob? You must have the cross-country chase?

Robert sits in the wicker chair

Robert Cut the location shots and you'll give Leo claustrophobia. He thinks television confined to studio sets is amateur stuff. And we won't get distribution abroad unless we can compete favourably with other series on the market.

Eva Where did you put my bag, Robert?

Maggy Oh, it's in my bedroom.

Robert (*rising*) Shall I get it?

Eva No—thank you.

Robert sits again. Eva goes into the bedroom, closing the door. She finds her bag on the dressing-table and applies lipstick. Then she glances furtively round the room before opening the dressing-table drawer and searching inside. She finds a few letters and begins to rifle through them with guilty haste. Meanwhile, the conversation in the lounge continues

Maggy So what's going to happen tomorrow? Have you two boys decided yet? Does Titania stay?

Peter Maggy, keep it to yourself. Even if it's true—and I still have my doubts—it certainly isn't common knowledge in this country.

Maggy Look, I don't care a damn for George's morals—they're *his* affair. But I just can't work with him, that's all.

Peter I've already told Leo I've got you both.

Maggy But you haven't got us both. It's either George—or me.

Robert If we start chopping and changing now it's going to take time and money.

Peter We've only hired the studio space for a limited period.

Robert And we can't keep the rest of the cast hanging around indefinitely.

Maggy In other words, we're off to a flying start. (*Rising*) I wonder if your wife needs anything, Robert?

Maggy goes to the bedroom door and starts to turn the handle. Eva, hearing the sound, glances over her shoulder, hastily replaces the letters and closes the drawer. The doorbell rings

Maggy goes into hall to answer the front door

Eva picks up her handbag and evening coat and goes into the lounge

Eva I'm ready, Robert, if you are.

Robert We don't want to arrive too early.

Eva You missed my luncheon party, so you're not doing me out of this evening.

Maggy enters with George Lawrence. He dresses quietly and though still good-looking, the ravages of drug addiction have left him tense, nervous; traits he attempts to cover up

George Hallo. Glad you're all here.

Eva is delighted to see George and goes to greet him with genuine warmth

Eva George, darling, how nice to see you. Robert and I were just on our way to a cocktail party but we'll stay a little longer now you've come.

Taking his hand, Eva leads George to the rocker, where she sits, and he remains standing beside her, smiling down at her

George Glad I caught you before you left, Eva. You look gorgeous.

Eva Thank you, George. (*She openly flirts with him, glancing over at Robert, trying to make him jealous*)

Maggy Tea, George, or would you prefer something stronger? (*She sits on the settee*)

George No, thanks, Maggy, I've just had tea at the Hilton—with my agent. I cut it short because Peter said you'd be having a meeting here.

Maggy It's practically over.

Eva Why don't you come to the cocktail party with us, George? The Becker-Scotts won't mind. Then you and I can talk in the back of the car. I'm so pleased you've agreed to be in the T.V. series. Do you like your part?

Robert sits on the basket chair

George Yes, very much.

Eva I'll persuade Robert to build you up in the next episode, make your role more important.

George kisses Eva on the cheek

George You're an angel, Eva.

Eva True, I am—in more senses than one.

George Oh, by the way, Maggy, I saw a friend of yours at the Hilton. He's staying there. Give you three guesses.

Maggy I never win at guessing games.

George Oh, it shouldn't be too difficult. Let me give you a clue. He's American, a big-league advertising executive—all the way from Madison Avenue . . .

Maggy puts down her cup with a clatter, staring out front

Well, do I need to spell it out for you?

George comes down level with Maggy, who slowly rises and looks at him disbelievingly. He nods, smiling

He asked after you. I gave him your address and telephone number. Did I do right?

Maggy picks up the hot-water jug and goes towards the kitchen

Maggy Of course. What else could you do?

Maggy exits into the kitchen

Robert Her husband?

George Yes—Ed Ryde. I saw him across the tea lounge. He recognized me and came over.

George moves to the mantelpiece and lights a small cigar, using the gold lighter there, which he fingers idly for a time before slipping it absently into his pocket

Eva I thought they were divorced. And if they're not, I'm sure he wouldn't have far to look for grounds. (*She glances meaningly at Robert*)

Peter Maggy left her husband a year ago in New York. It was just after the play closed.

George (*bitterly*) After he closed it, don't you mean? He had a lot of influence with the backer. (*Pause*) How did Maggy take it when you told her I was going to be in the series?

Peter Well, she didn't hang out any flags.

George So she's not too happy about the arrangement, then?

Eva (*going to him*) Why shouldn't she be? You'd make anyone a perfect leading man, George. (*She links her arm through his*)

George (*smiling at her*) Thanks, Eva, you're a darling. But I felt Maggy might be against working with me again. I wasn't too well in New York and she seemed to think *The Tiger* closed because of me.

Eva That's nonsense. How could it have been your fault?

George It wasn't, of course. We could have had a decent run if that damned backer hadn't let us down. It was only a question of keeping faith.

Eva I shall keep faith, George, darling, and I know you're going to be a great success.

Peter There are still a few problems to sort out. Could you all come round to my flat later on this evening?

Robert Yes, if you like. We'll try to get away from this cocktail party early. (*To Eva*) Do you like the idea, darling? We should hate you to be bored.

Eva Why should I be bored by going on to Peter's flat? You'll be discussing the series and I do happen to have a vested interest.

Maggy enters with the hot-water jug, followed by Mrs Dacre

Mrs Dacre I did explain when I came for the interview that I'd need time off for my shopping on Friday mornings. If I leave it till Saturday they put the prices up.

Maggy That's all right, you do your shopping tomorrow morning. More tea, anyone?

Murmurs of dissent from everyone. Maggy sits on the settee, puts more hot water into the teapot and pours herself another cup of tea

Mrs Dacre It will be after ten-thirty by the time I get here. Won't you be gone to rehearsal?

Maggy I'm not sure.
Mrs Dacre How will I get into the flat if you're gone?
Maggy I'll give you a key. I have a spare one.
Mrs Dacre Yes, that would be best, madam. Finished with the tray?

Maggy nods, retaining her cup and saucer

Mrs Dacre takes the tray into the kitchen, leaving the door open

Maggy finishes her tea and goes into the hall, opens her bag—which is still on the hall table, and takes out a key

Peter We're having a meeting at my flat later this evening, Maggy. Can you make it?
Maggy Wouldn't it be better if you talked things over without me?

The telephone rings. Maggy hesitates, with the key in her hand, then puts it on the hall table just out of view before she comes down to the telephone, calling towards the kitchen as she does so

I've left my spare key on the hall table, Mrs Dacre.
Mrs Dacre (*off*) Righto, madam.

Maggy lifts the receiver. George goes to the window

Eva If we're going to this cocktail party, Robert, let's make a move.
Maggy (*on the telephone*) Hallo. . . . Speaking. . . . Oh! Well, I can't talk just now. I have friends here. I'll call you back later. What's the number?

George is still at the window, peering out as Maggy replaces the receiver

George A traffic warden's coming down the street. He's going to spot your car, Robert.
Robert Right, let's get going. (*To Peter*) Can we give you a lift to your meter?
Peter No, I'll walk, could do with some fresh air.
Eva Good-bye, Miss Fairchild. I expect we shall be seeing each other again soon.
Maggy I hope so, Mrs Mallin.

Eva goes out, followed by Peter and Robert. They all brush against the hall table

George hovers

George (*to Maggy*) Anything wrong?

She avoids his gaze

You're disappointed because I'm going to be in the cast. I guessed you might be.
Maggy I'd rather not discuss it.
Robert (*off*) Buck up, George, I don't want a parking fine.
Maggy They're waiting for you.
George I need this part and I'm going to play it. So get used to the idea!

George goes out through archway, brushing against the hall table. Mrs Dacre enters from kitchen, wearing her hat and coat, and carrying a shopping-bag

Maggy notices that Robert has left his briefcase behind. She picks it up

Maggy Oh, Mr Mallin has forgotten this. Would you mind?

Mrs Dacre Yes, I'll take it to him. 'Bye, Miss Fairchild, I'll be round tomorrow. Leave a note if there's anything special you want me to do.

Mrs Dacre hurries into the hall as she speaks, carrying the briefcase

Maggy goes to the window, opens it and calls down

Maggy Robert, wait! Mrs Dacre is bringing your briefcase down. (*She waves, then closes the window and draws the curtains again, before going to the telephone and dialling. On the telephone*) The Hilton? . . . I'd like to speak to Mr Edward Ryde, please. Tell him it's his wife calling. (*She takes a cigarette from the box on the telephone table and lights it*)

Peter comes and stands watching silently from the hall

(*On the telephone*) Hallo, Ed, sorry I couldn't talk to you before. People were here. . . . Yes, they've gone now. . . . No, don't come round, I'll meet you. I think after a year you owe me a good dinner. (*She glances at her watch*) Around seven? . . . Oh, there's no need for you to do that. I can drive myself there. . . . Yes. Good-bye.

Maggy replaces the receiver and goes into the bedroom without noticing Peter. She draws the curtains at the window, then moves to the wardrobe and takes out a cocktail dress, carrying it down to the mirror. Peter comes just inside the bedroom doorway. Maggy turns in surprise

I thought you'd gone with the others.

Peter Your daily left the front door open. I came back to ask if you'd have dinner with me. But I gather you've already arranged to dine with some-one else.

Maggy throws the dress across the bed and goes to Peter

Maggy I have things to talk over with Ed. Another time, perhaps?

Peter nods, then puts his arms round her. She quickly extricates herself, smiling regretfully at him

Don't let's mix pleasure with business.

Peter Are you still carrying a torch for your husband?

Maggy If I am, the battery's very low. Good night, Peter.

Peter looks at her a little sadly, then turns and goes out. The front door slams

Maggy picks up the dress again, holding it against herself as she looks in the mirror

The Curtain is lowered to denote the passing of time until midnight

Midnight. Both rooms are in darkness, the curtains drawn. Arch curtains are open, revealing faint light from the hall

The front door slams, and Maggy enters, wearing the cocktail dress, a fur stole over her shoulders, carrying the same handbag used in the previous sequence

She appears tired as she switches on the main lights, then drops her fur and bag on the settee. She takes a cigarette from the box on the mantelpiece and lights up, looking thoughtful. She inhales for a few moments, then goes into the bedroom. Her housecoat is lying across the bed. She puts on the lamp, takes off her dress and puts on the housecoat. Then she returns to the lounge, goes to the wine cabinet, starts to pour herself a drink, changes her mind, goes into the kitchen and returns with a glass of milk. She switches off the hall light, comes into the lounge, closes the archway curtains and turns off the main lights before going into the bedroom. She puts the milk on the dressing-table, draws back the curtains, stubs out her cigarette, then picks up her dress and goes to the wardrobe to hang it up.

She pulls aside the sliding door, revealing—a figure in white Ku Klux Klan costume, hooded, with white boots and gauntlets. For a few moments she stares in horror at the apparition, then screams repeatedly. She backs away as the Figure leaps from the wardrobe and, gripping her by the throat, flings her across the bed. She is gasping and struggling wildly as—

the CURTAIN *falls*

ACT II

Scene 1

The same. Friday morning, nine o'clock

Pale sunlight streams through the bedroom window. The lamp is still on, the wardrobe door wide open

Maggy lies sideways across the bed, one hand falling limply over the edge. She is still in her housecoat. Her cocktail dress is on the floor. For some moments she remains perfectly immobile, then very slowly she begins to move, her hands clutching at the bedspread. Inch by inch she crawls to the top of the bed and sits up against the pillows, staring dazedly in front of her. There are livid blue marks on her throat. She puts a hand up to touch her neck and winces with pain. With considerable effort she manages to stand up and, supporting herself by holding on to the furniture and door, she reaches the lounge and the telephone. She leans on the table shakily then dials

Maggy (*on the telephone, huskily*) The Hilton? . . . Will you give a message to Mr Ed Ryde, please. . . . Tell him. . . . tell him it's very urgent. His wife wants him to come round to her flat at once. . . . Yes, at once. (*She crashes down the receiver, exhausted, then drops into the rocker and sits with her head in her hands for some moments*)

The doorbell rings. Maggy slowly looks up. Gradually she rises, reaches the settee and remains grasping it. The doorbell rings again.

With a further effort Maggy drags herself into the hall. Voices are heard off, then Mrs Dacre enters in hat and coat, carrying an empty shopping-bag. She is supporting Maggy, whom she leads down to the settee

Mrs Dacre Now you sit right there. I'm going to call a doctor. Who do you have—is it Dr Nichols? We ought to catch him before he goes out on his rounds.

Maggy I'm—I'm all right. I don't need—a doctor.

Mrs Dacre But you're ill. You gave me quite a turn when you opened the front door. What do you think it is—flu?

Maggy No, just a—sore throat.

Mrs Dacre (*staring down*) Madam, your neck!

Maggy puts a hand to her neck, then zips up the collar of her housecoat, hiding the bruises

Maggy I wound a scarf round it last night. I must have knotted it too tightly.

Mrs Dacre Fancy doing a thing like that. It's a wonder you didn't choke yourself. Oh, why don't you let me call a doctor? It never does to neglect yourself, you know,

Maggy Mrs Dacre, do you think you could make me some coffee, please?
Mrs Dacre Yes, of course. But do let me get the doctor first.
Maggy I'm all right, truly. I wouldn't dream of troubling him for a sore throat. I've phoned my husband, he'll be coming round soon.
Mrs Dacre Your husband? I thought he was in America.
Maggy What's the time?
Mrs Dacre (*looking at the clock*) Just after nine o'clock. I haven't done my shopping yet. I came straight here instead. Well, I thought if I didn't you'd be gone . . .
Maggy Gone?
Mrs Dacre To rehearsals. And I wouldn't be able to get in.
Maggy But I gave you a key.
Mrs Dacre Did you?

Mrs Dacre goes to the window and draws back the curtains, Sunlight streams in, lighting up the dim room

Maggy Yes, don't you remember? I left it on the hall table. You picked it up when you went out yesterday.
Mrs Dacre No, I never did. Wait a bit, I remember you calling out that you'd left a key for me . . . Oh, I am a silly. It was running after Mr Mallin with the briefcase that did it. I clean forgot all about the key. I suppose it must still be there. (*She draws the archway curtains back, goes into the hall and looks on the hall table*) No, not a sign of it. Are you sure you left it on the hall table?
Maggy Of course I'm sure.

Maggy notices her handbag, which has been on the settee with her fur all night. She opens the bag, tipping out the contents, and finding only one key. She holds it up as Mrs Dacre comes back into the room

Look, there's only this one and yesterday I had two. I distinctly remember taking out the other and placing it on the hall table.
Mrs Dacre Well, I'll have a good look round for it later. Now you rest there while I make the coffee.

Mrs Dacre exits to the kitchen

Maggy picks up her wallet and checks the number of pound notes inside. Then she puts everything back in the bag and takes it, together with her fur, into the bedroom. She puts out the lamp, then stands still, staring at the open wardrobe. Suddenly she stumbles towards it, crashing the door shut, and turns, leaning against it, sobbing quietly

Mrs Dacre, now in her overall, enters from the kitchen and crosses to the bedroom

Mrs Dacre Like some breakfast, would you? Nothing like a couple of back rashers for a sore throat.
Maggy No, I couldn't eat anything—just coffee.
Mrs Dacre Why don't you get back into bed? Turn on the electric blanket, make yourself comfortable. Honestly, you don't look a bit well.

Maggy I'm—all right, really I am.

Mrs Dacre Well, you won't be going to rehearsals today, that's a fact.

Mrs Dacre returns to the kitchen

Maggy looks at herself in the mirror. She brushes her hair, then unzips the top of her housecoat to look at her neck. She shudders and quickly fastens the zip

Slowly Maggy leaves the bedroom and goes off through the hall to the bathroom. Mrs Dacre enters with tray on which is a cup, saucer, spoon and sugar basin, which she places on the coffee-table, then goes into the hall, returning with the morning paper, letters and two bottles of milk. She pauses, looking towards the bathroom

You all right, madam?

Maggy (*off*) Yes, thank you.

Mrs Dacre Don't lock the door, in case you come over giddy.

Mrs Dacre comes to the coffee-table, drops the letters and papers on it, then takes the milk bottles into the kitchen

Pause. Doorbell rings

Mrs Dacre enters from the kitchen and goes to answer the front door

Ed (*off*) My name is Ed Ryde—Miss Maggy Fairchild's husband.

Mrs Dacre (*off*) Oh, come in, will you, sir?

Ed Ryde, an attractive American, a few years older than Maggy, enters with Mrs Dacre. Ed radiates success, authority, confidence, has a striking personality and a wry sense of humour

Mrs Dacre I've been so worried. I mean, she was fine yesterday and then to look like she did this morning. I wanted to call the doctor—but no, she wouldn't have him.

Ed Where is she?

Mrs Dacre (*pointing along the hall*) In the bathroom. I'm just making her some coffee. Perhaps you can persuade her to have the doctor, sir. She says it's only a sore throat but that could be the start of something serious, couldn't it? If you ask me, I think it's flu.

Ed How long will the coffee be?

Mrs Dacre Oh, you'd like a cup, I expect. Black, Mr Ryde? Most Americans like it black, don't they?

Ed I take mine white.

Mrs Dacre nods and goes into the kitchen

Ed moves to the hall and calls out:

Maggy, I just got here. Are you okay?

Maggy (*off*) Yes. I won't be a moment.

Ed comes into the lounge, glancing round him. He looks into the bedroom, then returns to the lounge and goes to the mantelpiece

Maggy enters from the hall

Ed (*going to her*) What is it, what's the trouble? Your hired help said you were sick. Shouldn't you be in bed?

Maggy (*passing him*) Last night—someone tried to—kill me! (*She drops on to the settee*)

Ed (*astounded*) *What* did you say?

Maggy I drove back here after we'd had dinner. I parked my car round the back, the way I always do—then I came in.

She closes her eyes. Ed sits beside her, putting a protective arm round her shoulders

Ed Take it easy, honey.

Maggy He was—hiding in the wardrobe. I went to hang up my dress and then—I was attacked. Look! (*She puts a hand to her throat and slowly unzips the collar, revealing the blue marks*)

Ed Some devil did that to you?

She nods, then zips up the collar

Mrs Dacre enters with a coffee-pot, extra cup and saucer and milk jug

Mrs Dacre He likes his coffee white, madam, so I've brought some milk. Now, sir, don't you think she ought to have the doctor? You can see for yourself she's all peaky.

Maggy I told you, Mrs Dacre. I'm all right.

Mrs Dacre Well, I don't know. If it was me I'd have the doctor like a shot, wouldn't you, sir?

Ed We can take care of this, thank you.

Mrs Dacre Like me to pour? (*She indicates the coffee-pot*)

Maggy No, we can manage. Mrs Dacre, why don't you go and do your shopping?

Mrs Dacre Will you be staying with her, sir? Because she needs someone.

Ed I'll be here.

Mrs Dacre Then if you don't mind I will pop off. I should do the lot in an hour and I'll be back to fix you some lunch.

Mrs Dacre goes into the kitchen

Ed pours the coffee and hands Maggy a cup

Ed Let me call the doc. I think he should take a look at you.

Maggy No, Ed, please. We mustn't have any bad publicity at this time. I'll explain after Mrs Dacre's gone. Give me a cigarette, will you?

Ed gives her a cigarette and lights it

Mrs Dacre enters in hat and coat with her shopping-bag

Mrs Dacre Any shopping I can do for you, madam?

Maggy No, thanks.

Mrs Dacre What about some throat pastilles?

Maggy I have plenty,

Mrs Dacre Then I'll be as quick as I can.

Mrs Dacre goes out through archway. The door slams

Ed turns on the electric fire, then goes behind the settee to the wine cabinet, picks up a bottle of brandy and tips a generous measure into Maggy's coffee-cup, which she holds out to him

Ed Who attacked you?

Maggy Someone disguised—wearing a sort of shroud, a shroud with a hood. You know, like that Secret Society in the States. What's it called now?

Ed The Ku Klux Klan?

Maggy Ye-es. Oh, it was horrible I opened the wardrobe door and it—leapt out at me. I remember screaming and screaming, then it caught me by the throat and I—I must have passed out.

Ed Didn't anyone hear you screaming? What about the people in the apartment below?

Maggy It's empty. I'm alone in the house.

Ed Well, what are we waiting for? This is a job for the police. (*He starts for the telephone*)

Maggy No, please, Ed, don't. Come and sit down. I told you I can't afford any bad publicity at this time. We've got to go carefully.

Ed (*moving to her*) Go carefully? What *is* this? You get yourself half strangled and then you talk of going carefully.

Maggy I don't want the police in on it.

Ed I don't care what you want. This is a police matter and we're going to turn it over to them.

Returning to the telephone, he lifts the receiver. Maggy jumps up, runs to him, takes the receiver away and bangs it down

Maggy I said no and I mean no! We're trying to do a deal with a big T.V. executive. If all this hits the papers he won't be interested any more. Everyone will think it's a stunt—they always do—and Leo hates stunts. Don't ask a lot of questions now, but that's the way it is.

Maggy returns to the settee. Ed strolls round to the window

Ed How did he get in?

Maggy I don't know. There isn't any way into this flat except through the front door.

Ed No fire escape?

Maggy shakes her head. Ed examines the catches on the closed windows

Anything been stolen—money, your jewellery?

Maggy Most of my jewellery's in the bank. I only keep a few trinkets here. And my handbag wasn't touched. All my money is still there. I checked to make sure.

Ed No catches broken. Was the window closed last night?

Maggy Yes, and the curtains were drawn. My bedroom window has bars, so do all the other windows up here.

Ed walks into the bedroom

Where are you going?

Ed Just checking. (*From the bedroom*) Maggy . . .

She goes into bedroom

Make sure all your jewellery is intact.

She goes to the dressing-table and opens her jewel-box, while he searches around for clues, opening the wardrobe door and pushing aside clothes. He investigates the window. All this is done very quickly

Maggy Everything seems to be here. Perhaps his motive wasn't robbery.

Ed Unless he panicked and dived off before helping himself. But that still leaves the big question-mark: how did he get into the apartment?

Maggy (*staring out front, thoughtfully*) There was a key—a front-door key. I put it on the hall table for Mrs Dacre, but . . .

Ed But what?

Maggy She forgot to pick it up. She left in rather a hurry. Robert had forgotten his briefcase and she ran after him with it.

Ed And the key's gone?

Maggy Yes. We looked for it this morning but there was no sign. You see, the others went out before Mrs Dacre. Anyone could have picked up that key if they'd wanted to.

She moves back into the lounge. Ed follows

Ed Who knew you were going to be out last night?

Maggy Only Peter Clinton. He came back while I was phoning you. He wanted me to have dinner with him.

Ed And is this guy the jealous type?

Maggy I wouldn't have said so.

Ed We're making progress. Whoever got into the apartment had a key. Have you handed out a front-door key to anyone in the past?

Maggy No. That lock was changed a month ago and I only had two keys cut.

Ed So Mrs Dacre doesn't take the key, but someone else does. Someone who figures on returning and letting himself in. Let's start at the beginning. Who hates you around town or—who loves you?

Maggy I don't know.

Ed This T.V. project—what's the deal?

Maggy We had a read-through yesterday and afterwards Peter, Robert and George came here for a discussion. (*She sits on the settee*) Peter Clinton is producing and directing, Robert Mallin is writing the scripts, and George Lawrence is hoping to play the lead.

Ed Anyone else?

Maggy Oh, yes, Eva Mallin. She's Robert's wife and her money is financing the scheme.

Ed Was there any trouble—friction?

Maggy Well, I did tell Peter and Robert that I wouldn't work with George Lawrence again.

Ed George Lawrence—the same fairy who played opposite you on
Broadway?

Maggy Yes.

Ed So yesterday you had the four of them here and, on leaving, someone
picked up that key from the hall table.

Maggy Oh, it's ridiculous. It couldn't be any of them. I know George has
never liked me—he has his reasons—but surely that's no excuse for
murder.

Ed How about the other three?

Maggy Peter wouldn't do anything crazy. Besides he wants this series to be
a success. Come to that, so does Robert—anything, I should imagine,
to be independent of his nagging wife.

Ed She's loaded?

Maggy Her father is. He's a soap millionaire.

Ed Well, if you won't have the police in on this then there's no alternative.
I move in.

Maggy Wh-at?

Ed sits beside her

Ed Wipe that shocked expression from your lovely face, Maggy. I'm still
your husband. Only I'll be here strictly as a bodyguard. Someone wants
you dead, so either you get your Scotland Yard to take over, or *I* do.
And just in case of emergencies you'd better learn to use this.

*He takes a small automatic from his pocket. Maggy rises, staring at the
weapon in alarm*

Maggy This is England . . .

Ed Then I'll see you're buried in a Union Jack.

Maggy But people don't . . .

Ed They don't carry guns around the way they do umbrellas? Pity. Or
maybe they prefer to use their hands—when it comes to a killing? (*He
offers her the gun*)

Maggy (*shuddering*) I couldn't.

Ed You can and you will, if it's necessary.

He presses it into her hand. She looks down at it with horror

Maggy I'd never have the courage.

Ed It's easy when it's either you or the other guy.

Maggy throws the gun on the settee with distaste

Maggy I'm supposed to be going to rehearsals.

Ed Cancel. Phone them and say you have a sore throat and can't make it.
No other details. (*He takes a small notebook and a Biro from his pocket*)
I'll have a list of those names again, just for the record. Peter Clinton,
T.V. producer, Robert Mallin, script writer, George Fairy Lawrence . . .

Maggy And Eva Mallin.

Ed What's she got against you?

Maggy Mrs Mallin? Nothing that I know of. But then no one really has

anything against me. There must be some other explanation. Ed, you
don't want to be involved in all this. I know I sent for you when I came
round but I didn't know what else to do. I was panicky and confused.
Still, I'm all right now. I'll get dressed, I'll go to rehearsals . . .

Maggy goes into bedroom. Ed follows

Ed I *am* involved, Maggy, I'll always be involved, so let's say no more
about that.

Maggy I don't want you to be sorry for me. Last night we were talking
about a divorce.

Ed *You* were talking about it, *I* wasn't.

Maggy I just want to wait a little longer. Divorce is something else Leo is
against.

Ed Bully for Leo!

Maggy Once the series is launched and we have contracts, then you and I
can come to some arrangement.

He returns to the lounge. She follows

Ed You walked out on me, Maggy, I didn't walk out on you. And my
visit to this country wasn't strictly for business purposes. Now you
have a choice—the protection of the police—or my protection. Maybe
you prefer the police. (*He goes to the telephone*) I think one dials
nine-nine-nine . . .

He is about to lift the receiver when Maggy stops him

Maggy There's a spare room across the hall, if you're determined to stay
here.

Ed Okay. Now when you feel fit enough you can come over to the Hilton
with me while I collect my baggage and check out. I don't want you
sticking around this apartment on your own. And get this straight—
you're not going to rehearsals today, that's for sure.

The telephone rings. Maggy and Ed exchange glances, then she lifts receiver

Maggy (*on the telephone*) Hallo, Maggy Fairchild speaking . . . Hallo. . . .
Hallo, who is that? . . . Will you please tell me who you are? . . . Why
don't you speak?

Ed comes to her side, takes the receiver and listens, he replaces it

Ed They've hung up. (*Pause*) Someone checking, Maggy—to see if you're
still alive.

Maggy shivers and Ed places a comforting arm round her shoulders

A silent caller at the other end of the line—a silent, would-be killer. This
morning he must be a very disappointed guy. That means he'll have to—
try again.

Maggy puts a hand to her throat, as—

the CURTAIN *falls*

SCENE 2

The same. Friday night

Maggy is in the bedroom wearing a glamorous, white nightdress with a housecoat over it. She sits at the dressing-table, brushing her hair

Ed enters lounge from hall. He is in pyjamas and dressing-gown. He pauses outside the bedroom door and taps

Ed You okay, Maggy?
Maggy Yes, thank you, Ed. (*Pointedly*) Good night.

Ed hesitates reluctantly, then shrugs and starts to move back to the archway. Maggy removes her housecoat, throws it across the stool, and gets into bed. Ed turns back and taps on the door again

Ed Care for a night-cap?
Maggy No, thanks. But you help yourself to anything you want.

A gleam comes into Ed's eyes and he opens the door and comes into the bedroom with alacrity. Maggy sits up in bed, her expression cool

   It's late.
Ed Not all that late.
Maggy Isn't the spare bed comfortable?
Ed I wouldn't know, I haven't tried it yet. Aw, come on, let's talk. Seems a pity to waste time sleeping.

He sits on the edge of the bed, taking Maggy's hand. She slips hastily out of bed, though he still holds her hand, turning to face her

   I wouldn't sleep easy, not while there are so many things to figure out.
Maggy Haven't we gone over it all enough times?
Ed But if we keep talking it out we might come up with something. Now let's think—how would the police tackle this?
Maggy Not with finger-prints—he wore gloves.
Ed But he must have made a slip—they always do.
Maggy So you mean to play detective?
Ed Someone has to. It's our responsibility to find out who it is and turn 'em over to the police.
Maggy And the police would take our word for it?
Ed Why not? If we had proof?
Maggy Scotland Yard men don't care for amateur detectives.
Ed Don't you want to know?
Maggy Of course I want to know.
Ed Even if it happens to be one of your friends, someone you like a whole lot, someone you may even think you love?

Maggy pulls her hand away and walks up to the stool. She puts on her housecoat

Maggy I can't imagine a Scotland Yard inspector asking me that.

Ed lies full-length on the bed, leaning against the pillows, facing front, ankles crossed

Ed I'm in dead earnest, even if *you're* not.

Maggy And now you're about to mount a campaign. You'll bring all your business ability to bear on the case. What is it they call you on Madison Avenue? The Instant Man in Advertising—the quick-thinker, the guy who comes up with the answer while the others are still putting the questions . . .

Ed This time *I'm* putting the questions.

Maggy Then fire away. But hours from now I doubt if we'll be one step nearer a solution.

Ed Have fun, make light of it—only when you have a moment just write your Last Will and Testament.

Maggy (*shivering*) You say the nicest things.

Ed (*sitting up*) Tell me about these people. Peter Clinton. You say you've known him a long time. Okay, fill me in with the details. What's his background? Is he married?

Maggy No. And why do we have to start with Peter? He's very fond of me. In fact he wants me to divorce you and marry him.

Ed Charming! I'm getting to like him less and less.

Maggy Still, you can rule him out of your suspects. He'd never want to harm me.

Ed Don't be so sure. Love can turn to hate, especially after he knew I was back on the scene. A jealous man is capable of anything.

Maggy He might want to kill *you*, but not—oh, you've got an obsession about Peter.

Ed (*rising*) True, I've got an obsession—and it's about the joker who tried to snuff you out last night. Peter Clinton, someone else, who knows? But I intend to find out and come up with the answer before the weekend's through.

Maggy Good luck.

Maggy strolls into the lounge. Ed follows

Ed If you hold out on me then I don't have a prayer. But I'll tell you one thing—if the Chinese boxes don't fit by Monday morning then Scotland Yard can take over. And I mean that.

Maggy But Leo will get to hear.

Ed goes to her, wagging his finger mock-threateningly

Ed Just you mention that guy Leo once more as a reason for shielding a would-be killer—then, by heck, I'll forget all I ever said about never hitting a woman!

Maggy (*amused*) You wouldn't dare!

Ed (*teasingly*) Wanna bet?

She smiles, shrugs and moves away

Maggy All right, what do you want to know?

Ed Details of Peter Clinton.

Maggy He was once a successful T.V. producer. Everything went marvellously at first. He couldn't do a thing wrong, and then suddenly he couldn't do a thing right. He was out. Finished. (*She sits in the rocker and turns to face Ed*)

Ed No scandal?

Maggy I never heard of anything.

Ed What effect did failure have on him?

Maggy After a time he had to start borrowing from his friends.

Ed How much did you lend him?

Maggy swings the chair round to face front. Ed swings her back

And he never repaid you?

Maggy As soon as Peter's established again he'll square things.

Ed How long has he been out of favour?

Maggy About three years. He hasn't worked in T.V. for ages. Then six months ago he was ill . . .

Ed What kind of illness?

Maggy swings the rocker round to face front again. Ed strides away impatiently to the fireplace

We're getting no place fast.

Maggy (*rising*) He had a breakdown and went into hospital—as a voluntary patient.

Ed The psychiatric ward?

Maggy Thousands of people have breakdowns. Don't jump to all the wrong conclusions.

Ed How sick was he?

Maggy He was very depressed and unhappy. I went to see him often. They kept him in hospital for about three months, then he got better and went on a cruise.

Ed I see.

Maggy No, you don't see anything. He wasn't out of his mind, he was just run down.

Ed Oh, sure.

Maggy It's true. And after the way people had treated him I wasn't surprised. (*She moves about the room tensely*) Ed, it's hard for you to understand. We haven't all got your resilience to life and failure. Failure is a devil. In time it makes you sink until you don't believe there's a straw to cling to.

Ed You speak from experience?

Maggy Yes, I speak from experience. I've had a whole year to do an awful lot of thinking. (*She goes over to Ed*) It isn't easy when you've once been in demand, with star-billing everywhere, and then managements don't seem anxious to book you. The phone doesn't ring the way it once did. Your photograph is still in *Spotlight*, but producers turn two pages at once.

Ed So that's what you and Peter have in common—an affinity to each other because you've both been kicked around.

Maggy I haven't been kicked around the way Peter has. It's worse for a man—all authority gone, all status lost in the only profession he knows. In my case I had to live down that Broadway disaster, and while people seldom manage to recall your successes, they have an uncanny knack of remembering your failures. (*She drops on to the settee, leaning back wearily*)

Ed You never have stopped blaming me for the closure of the Broadway show.

Maggy I think you helped to put up the shutters.

Ed (*sitting beside her*) Have I ever denied the fact? Still, we don't intend to cover that ground again. The episode is over.

Maggy It may be over, Ed, like a lot of things are over, but it leaves a recurring bad taste.

Ed Any time this past year you could have come back, you know that.

Maggy I didn't intend to crawl. First I wanted to prove that I could get by on my own. Now it's your turn to laugh.

Ed I make a point of laughing only when it's funny. Now I want to know something of the background of all these friends of yours. For the time being we've packaged Peter Clinton. Unstable character, who doesn't care to be rejected. How often have you rejected him personally?

Maggy (*rising and leaning on the mantelpiece*) Peter and I were never more than—just good friends.

Ed In show business that can mean anything.

Maggy (*reacting*) We got together with Robert Mallin to push this pilot episode, so naturally we've seen rather a lot of each other lately.

Ed How about this author guy?

Maggy Robert was little more than an acquaintance before we started to discuss the project.

Ed He was in New York when you were in *The Tiger*. I saw him backstage and you introduced us.

Maggy Lots of people come backstage. Robert was there to congratulate George and me. It might have been better if he'd commiserated.

Ed His wife didn't go over with him, did she?

Maggy No, I met Eva Mallin at a party at their house.

Ed The lady with this mink-lined bank account?

Maggy Yes. I'm sure that's one of the reasons why Robert was so desperate to get into T.V. If only he could become financially independent he might have the courage to walk out.

Ed (*rising*) And leave a million bucks behind? Not a chance. Has Robert Mallin anything against you?

Maggy No, why on earth should he have?

Ed I'm asking the questions. Think, and think hard.

Maggy If Robert didn't like me he needn't have suggested me for the series.

Ed How about this George Lawrence? (*moving around*) A junkie, a compulsive drinker—and a queer. Dispose of leading lady and the road is clear ahead. The producer and the author would have to find a substitute and the next choice might be an actress who admires George. Is that the picture you frame?

Maggy Could be. He told me things about himself when we were in New York, things he must have bitterly regretted when he sobered up. Oh, but Ed, he hasn't the guts. (*She puts feet up on the settee*)

Ed Weak characters often do amazing things. Now what about the woman?

Maggy Eva Mallin? She doesn't really like me. Some women don't like their own sex on principle. But that's hardly an excuse for murder. We might just as well put all the names into a hat, shuffle them around, then draw one out.

Ed Four people—one stolen key—and a Ku Klux Klan outfit.

Maggy Even if we do discover who it is, what do we do then?

Ed Hand him—or her—over to the police.

Maggy And raise a storm of publicity?

Ed lifts her legs, sits beside her, and, placing her ankles across his lap, caresses them affectionately as he talks

Ed Your friend Leo won't be able to condemn you for it. He'll know then it wasn't a stunt. Of course, if it turns out to be Robert Mallin you can hardly go on acting his script and using his wife's money for the venture.

Maggy And if it's Peter?

Ed You could find another producer, I guess.

Maggy Oh, Ed, let's drop it all. I want to do this T.V. series . . .

Ed I never heard of an actress being a success from the morgue.

Maggy He won't try again.

Ed I shouldn't lay any bets on that. Now the first thing I want to know is: where did he get the costume?

Maggy It could have been hired. Or a woman could have made it herself.

Ed I doubt it. Whoever did this had that outfit at the ready.

Maggy How do you know?

Ed Simple. First they steal your spare key, then they pounce the very same night. Where's the time to go hiring or making a Klan outfit? No, they either had it by them or picked it up somewhere at a moment's notice. Right then—tomorrow morning we ring round to theatrical costumiers and ask if they ever rent Ku Klux Klan outfits.

Maggy And if they do, what will that prove?

Ed It might give us a lead to the would-be killer.

The doorbell rings. Ed and Maggy exchange startled glances

Expecting the mortician?

Maggy Who'd be calling at this hour of night?

The doorbell rings again. Maggy starts for the hall. Ed draws her back

Ed Hold it.

Maggy Why?

Ed He may have a key—remember?

They stand together, waiting

Who knows I've moved in here?

Maggy No-one, apart from Mrs Dacre. But if he has my spare key, why ring the doorbell?

Ed As a precautionary measure. Can the lights up here be seen from the street?

Maggy Not when the curtains are drawn. They're so thickly lined that it's a complete back-out.

The doorbell rings more insistently

Ed Okay, I'll get it.

Ed goes out to the hall

Maggy moves to the fireplace, looking anxious

There is a murmur of voices, then Ed enters with George

George Hope I didn't get you up. I couldn't see any light from outside, but I chanced it.

Maggy Hallo, George. I think you know my husband.

George Yes, of course. So you didn't find the hotel so comfortable, Mr Ryde?

Ed The hotel was fine. The company here is more attractive.

George Oh, I see. Maggy, are you feeling better?

Maggy Yes, thanks, George. It was only a sore throat, but I didn't think I ought to strain it at rehearsals.

George I really called in because when I was here yesterday I picked up something of yours by mistake, Maggy.

Maggy and Ed exchange glances

So as I was quite near here tonight I thought I'd look in and return it.

Maggy You picked up something of mine, George?

George That's right. Stupid of me. I must have jackdaw tendencies.

Ed What was it?

George (*searching his pockets*) I've got it here somewhere. I suppose you missed it, Maggy?

Maggy We-ell . . .

George Ah! (*He takes the lighter from his pocket*) One gold cigarette lighter.

Maggy Oh!

George Sentimental as well as intrinsic value, I suspect. Inscribed: "From Ed to Maggy with love".

Maggy Thank you George. (*She takes the lighter. Slowly*) You didn't, by any chance, pick up anything else while you were here?

George No, why? Is something else missing?

Ed My wife was joking. Like a drink?

George No, thanks. Actually I've just come from a party. It was pretty awful. A bottle of Scotch was smashed and I can still smell the stuff. I'm on the wagon, you see, have been for a long time. (*He is anxious for them to know this*) If you're not too tired, Maggy, I was wondering if we could have a little talk.

Maggy What do you want to talk about, George? (*She sits on the settee*)

George It's private. (*He looks pointedly at Ed*)

Ed If it concerns my wife, then it concerns me.

George I don't think it does. It's about Maggy's career and you wouldn't be interested in that.

Ed Try me.

George In New York you were damned glad when the play folded.

Ed Are you sure you haven't been drinking?

Maggy Ed, please.

George It's all right, Maggy. I know everyone blames me for the shutdown of *The Tiger*. Only we know differently, don't we?

Maggy Do we?

George Your husband persuaded his partner to take off the show, withdraw his backing.

Ed He was not only my partner, he was also my friend, and I wasn't going to stand by and watch Chuck drain away thousands more dollars just for the sake of the actors' egos.

George He mightn't have lost his money. We needed to establish ourselves. Things are often a little shaky at first. I know I wasn't well and that's why I couldn't give my best to the part. But I'd have got better if only your friend Chuck had nursed the play.

Ed Why should he be your wet nurse?

George glares at Ed, then sits beside Maggy

George Maggy, isn't it possible for us to work together again? When we got the message this morning at rehearsal I guessed your sore throat was merely diplomatic.

Maggy (*rising*) Oh?

George Because of me. You don't want me in the cast, do you?

Maggy Face it, George, we don't work well together. (*She sits in the basket chair*)

George I know I've a lot to live down. It's difficult to bury your failures in this profession. Someone always remembers and they're not slow to hold it against you. One unfortunate performance, one bit of bad luck, and you might as well shut up shop.

Ed It's an idea.

George (*rounding on Ed*) What do you know about it? The powerful boss of a successful advertising agency, an agency that uses all its persuasion tricks to hoodwink the public into buying trash!

Ed (*sitting in the rocker*) No-one buys what they don't want, brother, but for the record we're not discussing *my* methods.

George (*rising*) You think I ought to quit, don't you; but I'm not a man with a university degree who can suddenly turn his hand to something else. I'm an actor and all I need is the right break.

Ed If this is going to be a sob story, hold on while I get my Kleenex.

Maggy (*rising*) Ed . . .

Ed He cried on your shoulder once before, Maggy, and this looks like being a repeat performance.

Maggy George, I'm sorry about everything, but the fact remains that—well, you don't inspire me with confidence. It wouldn't be fair to either of us if we tried to work together again.

George (*sitting on the settee*) Give me a trial, Maggy. I won't let you down. I swear to God I won't.

Maggy I need time to think it over.

George Yes, you do that. (*He turns to Ed*) I'll have that drink now, Mr Ryde.

Ed (*rising*) I thought you said . . .

George A bitter lemon.

Ed (*amused*) Oh, sure. (*He goes to pour the drink*)

George It wasn't true, Maggy—all I said to you in your dressing-room at the theatre. I was upset after the Butchers of Broadway had made it a personal slaughter. I made a lot of excuses and told you a few lies about my private life, pretending I had some special men friends, but of course I'm not like that really. I'd been drinking, I didn't realize what I was saying.

Ed (*grinning as he hands him his glass*) One bitter lemon.

George gives him a look, takes the drink, sips it, then turns pleadingly to Maggy

George So may I ring Peter tomorrow and say we've decided?

Maggy What have we decided, George?

George To forget the past. Look, we're going to rehearse for a fortnight, then film the episode and if, after that, you want me to back down—all right, I'll do so. But at least give me a chance to prove I can pull my weight.

Ed How can that prove anything, son? If you land the rest of the series, it will mean plenty of hard work, plenty of staying power. Do you think you'll match up?

George rises, slamming his glass down on the mantelpiece

George What the hell has it got to do with you? I didn't come here to ask *your* opinion! That's the last thing I'd ever want after what you did. You set out to ruin Maggy's career and you damn near succeeded. All that rubbish about wanting her to be a success. Maggy, your husband persuaded his partner to close the Broadway show, and I can tell you why. He thought you'd be so disillusioned, so sick of everything that you'd be ready to quit the profession and be plain Mrs Ed Ryde.

Ed smiles tolerantly and sits in the rocker

He's probably trying to talk you out of this T.V. scheme right now. What does he care about your career, what has he ever cared?

Ed You're getting excited, is it good for you?

George (*glaring*) All the while Maggy was out of work you stayed away. Now there's this chance you arrive hot foot to scotch it. Ask him, Maggy, ask him if it isn't true. At the party tonight I was talking to someone who said he knew Ed Ryde very well. They flew over together a few days ago, and your devoted husband knew just about everything—all you've been doing this past year, the T.V. set-up, your friends, the lot!

Ed Slow down, sonny, you're racing your engine.

George He likes being the big ad-man, who only has to lift one of his dozen telephones to get every answer he wants. (*To Ed*) How many spies have you put on her trail these past months?

Ed Only 007. (*He swivels round to face front, avoiding the accusation in Maggy's eyes*)

George I know why you wanted to smash up Maggy's career. You couldn't bear the thought of being known as "Mr Fairchild". It didn't fit the image, did it? Maggy Fairchild's husband—not Ed Ryde, the envy of all the other Madison Avenue go-getters—one of the great persuaders. But the one person you couldn't persuade was Maggy and oh, how that damaged your ego!

Maggy George, you can't blame Ed for *our* disagreement. I didn't even know he was in this country when I said I'd rather not—well . . .

Ed (*rising*) That she'd rather not work with you again. That still stands, and I doubt if she'll think differently by Monday morning.

George Because you mean to persuade her over the week-end. Well, I'll tell you both something you can mull over when I've gone. If I don't play in this T.V. series, then I'll make sure nobody does. Get that?

Ed I guess you know your own way out.

Pause. Ed moves towards George

Or do you need any help?

George glares at Ed, then strides out. The front door slams

Maggy rises, her expression cool

Maggy *Did* you know about the T.V. idea? Yes, of course you knew. Just how many private detectives have you employed to keep track of my activities?

Ed You don't believe all the rattletrap that junkie talked, surely? I figured you had a higher I.Q.

Maggy How much did it cost you to have me trailed, or did that come under the heading of expenses?

Ed It wasn't that way at all. If a friend had been to London then naturally I'd ask if he'd seen or heard anything of you. You were on my mind. I wanted to be sure you were okay.

Maggy George touched on the truth tonight. You don't want me to work, you've never wanted me to. Nothing would please you more than for me to throw up everything and go back to the States with you.

Ed That's right. Nothing would please me more.

Maggy Then you're going to be disappointed. I'm carrying on with the series—even if I'm forced to have *George Lawrence* in the cast!

She pushes past Ed and goes into the bedroom. He follows her to the doorway

Ed It's your life—what's left of it. Because one person is going to make darned sure you never play anything.

She stares at him

Maggy Good night!

She slams the door and locks it, as

the CURTAIN *falls*

SCENE 3

The same. Saturday morning

The remains of breakfast are on the coffee-table, along with the morning paper

Ed, in casual clothes, is speaking on the telephone. He sits in the rocker, the telephone on his lap. On the floor is a copy of the "Stage", a notepad and Biro, and a coffee-cup. Maggy is in the bedroom, wearing a pink trouser-suit. She is examining her bruises critically in the mirror. She picks up a brown chiffon scarf and arranges it round her neck to cover the bruises. For the remainder of the play she wears various little scarves to cover up these marks

Ed (*on the telephone*) I'd be glad if you'd call me back when he comes in. You've got this number, haven't you?... Right, good-bye. (*He replaces receiver and calls out*) Marvells are going to phone me back when the manager gets in. They say they haven't a Klan outfit for hire at the moment, but they did make one not long ago.

Maggy Who for?

Ed They couldn't tell me. I think they have it on record but you know what it is. They don't like to commit themselves in case it gets them in bad with the manager. It's up to him to decide whether to give me their client's name.

Maggy comes into the lounge

Maggy Do you think he will?

Ed Maybe. I made it all sound very innocuous—just that I wanted it for a fancy dress ball and hoped they might rent it out to me. Now we wait and see if they call me back.

Maggy (*picking up his cup from the floor*) More coffee?

Ed Thanks.

Maggy (*going to the settee*) You must have run out of theatrical costumiers. How many did you ring?

Ed Five. That was the last one on my list. All the others said they'd never had a call for a Klan outfit. Not surprising. It isn't the sort of thing I'd care to wear at a social function. (*He rises, yawning and stretching*)

Maggy (*handing him his coffee*) Tired?

Ed M'm. I didn't sleep too well.

Maggy Wasn't the bed comfortable?

Ed The bed was okay, I guess, but I was cold and lonesome, knowing you were so near and yet so far. Are you still mad at me?

Maggy What do *you* think?

Ed Well, I don't get you. Why are you wild at me just 'cos that psycho

character, George Lawrence, blew his stack last night? The way you
soaked it all up. Do you really believe I'm that kind of a heel?

Maggy Convince me otherwise.

Ed I thought I had. Maybe I did come over with the idea of persuading
you to return to New York with me, but what's so bad about that? If I
could have gotten away sooner I would have done. I wrote you three
times a week, care of the Arts Club, but how often did you bother to
reply?

Maggy Perhaps I had nothing to say.

Ed The cold, silent Maggy Fairchild.

Maggy If someone tried to stop you working, how would you feel?

Ed I never tried to stop you doing a single thing. That play hadn't a
snowball's chance in hell.

Maggy We might have saved it with a new leading man.

Ed Quit stalling, Maggy, George was bad, heaven knows, but even
Richard Burton couldn't have saved that show. Still, that's all washed
up now. Let's get wise to ourselves. We had a good marriage, we can
still have a good marriage. All it needs is for us both to stop behaving
like a couple of high school kids with dark grievances. (*Gently*) I happen
to love you very much.

She turns her head to look at him

Otherwise I wouldn't be here. And you love me. If you didn't you'd
have gotten a divorce—

Maggy rises abruptly and takes a cigarette from the box on the mantelpiece

—and started shacking up with Peter Clinton.

Maggy (*facing front*) Would I really?

Ed rises, moving behind her

Ed Sure you would. You're the kind of woman who needs a man around.
Have you forgotten the way it was with us? We had seven good years,
seven very happy years—until that show loused things up for us (*He
lights her cigarette*) Still, we'll go into all that later. Right now we've got
other things on our minds (*Moving away*) Now this evening we're going
to throw a little party.

Maggy I'm not in the mood for parties.

Ed goes into the bedroom to fix his tie at the mirror

Ed This won't be an ordinary party. Just a handful of people—four
people, in fact. Four suspects. We're going to give them a drink and then
tell them what happened to you on Thursday night.

Maggy (*startled, going to the bedroom door*) Tell them?

Ed Sure. Oh, we'll change the story around to suit our purposes. We'll
say someone broke into the apartment and attacked you and you were
all alone. You believe the motive was robbery. You didn't go ahead and
inform the police in case it looked like an organised stunt to gain
publicity.

Ed returns to the lounge

Maggy And what is my official reason for calling them together?

Ed I'm coming to that. You're still a little shaken up, suffering after effects from that bad experience. You'd appreciate it if they'd hold back rehearsals for a short while. You need to take a week's vacation. Where do you have any relations?

Maggy I have an Aunt in Brighton.

Ed Right. Say you're going down to Brighton tomorrow morning. I have to leave for Scotland this evening on urgent business. So for one night— you are going to be on your own.

Maggy Am I?

Ed I'm not really going any place. That's the switch.

Maggy But what's the point?

Ed The point, honey, is that for one night it will look as if you're here alone, vulnerable, unprotected. And that zombie isn't going to miss a chance like that. Not when he wants you dead.

Maggy (*picks up the telephone from the floor*) I'll ring round and invite them for eight o'clock . . .

Ed Yeah, but not just yet. I want the line left clear for Marvells. They've promised to ring me back about that Klan outfit.

Maggy Oh, yes. (*She puts the telephone on the bureau*) Do you really think he'll stage a repeat performance?

Ed I doubt if he'll change his tactics. But in any case—we'll be waiting.

Mrs Dacre enters from kitchen with dusters

Mrs Dacre Will it be all right if I clean round now, Miss Fairchild? I won't be staying long, as it's Saturday.

Maggy Yes, all right, Mrs Dacre.

Mrs Dacre moves round the room, dusting. Ed stands by the mantelpiece, reading the paper

Mrs Dacre Is your sore throat any better now, madam?

Maggy Oh, yes, it's fine, thanks.

Maggy goes into the bedroom to tidy herself. Mrs Dacre comes to the bedroom door to chat as she dusts the wine cabinet

Mrs Dacre Then I expect you'll be going to rehearsals on Monday.

Maggy I'm not sure yet.

Mrs Dacre I shall need a key to get in if you do go to rehearsal, won't I? Funny where that other one got to. Did you ever find it?

Maggy No, I didn't.

Mrs Dacre I've done the hall thoroughly since then and there wasn't a sign of it.

She goes behind the settee to address Ed, who has his back to her

Miss Fairchild lost a key, sir, did she tell you?

Ed Uh? Oh, yup.

Mrs Dacre It's a proper mystery where it's got to. (*She goes to the bedroom door to call out again to Maggy*) Now your husband's staying he'll want a key won't he? I could get you another one cut, madam—another two, if you like. There's a place in the High Street that does it while you wait.

Maggy (*entering the lounge*) No, don't bother. The other one is sure to turn up sometime.

The telephone rings. Ed drops the paper, snaps his fingers to Maggy signalling her to get rid of Mrs Dacre, strides over to the telephone and lifts the receiver. Maggy urges Mrs Dacre towards the hall

Maggy (*quickly*) Mrs Dacre, would you make Mr Ryde's bed now? I'll help you to turn the mattress.

Ed lifts the receiver, impatiently waiting for Mrs Dacre to go

Mrs Dacre His bed? Oh! didn't he . . .? (*She looks towards Maggy's room*)

Maggy He slept in the spare room.

Mrs Dacre Well, I never!

Maggy succeeds in getting Mrs Dacre off into the hall and follows her, closing the curtains behind them

Ed (*on the telephone*) Hallo. . . . That's right. . . . Kind of you to call me back. . . . Yes, I do need the costume in rather a hurry, so if you could give me the name of your client, maybe I could borrow it from him. . . . (*Pause, then slowly*) Yes, I've got the name and the phone number, do you know it? (*He scribbles it down in his notebook*) I'm most grateful for all your trouble, Good-bye. (*He replaces the receiver and stands staring out front thoughtfully. Then he glances at his notebook again, lifts the receiver and dials*) Oh, hallo. Ed Ryde here—Maggy Fairchild's husband. Could I speak to Mr . . .? . . . I see. Well, maybe you can help me. I've been invited to a fancy dress ball at short notice and I don't have a thing with me to wear. Miss Fairchild seems to remember that he once had a fancy dress costume. . . . He has? Well, that's fine. I wonder if he could lend it to me? Would you ask him, please, when he comes in? And would you also mention that Miss Fairchild is having a small party this evening at around eight o'clock. It's to discuss the T.V. project. . . . Many thanks. Good-bye. (*He replaces receiver. Excitedly he strides up and calls out*) Maggy, can you come in here a moment? (*He goes to the mantelpiece*)

Maggy enters

Maggy Yes?

Ed You're not going to like this, honey. They made a Klan outfit three months ago . . .

Maggy Who for?

Ed The guy you lent money to, the guy whose hand you held when he was sick . . .

Maggy (*stunned*) Not—Peter?

Ed Yeah—Peter Clinton.

CURTAIN

ACT III

Scene 1

The same. Saturday, shortly before 8 p.m.

Maggy enters from the kitchen with a bowl of ice-cubes and two dishes of peanuts. She puts the ice on the wine cabinet, one bowl of peanuts on the bureau and another on the mantelpiece. Ed comes into the hall from the spare bedroom with a leather hold-all, which he places outside the archway, throwing his sheepskin coat over it. He enters the room

Ed How long before they arrive?

Maggy About five minutes. I asked them to be here sharp at eight, if possible.

Ed Let's have a pre-party drink. (*He goes to the wine cabinet and pours*) How do you feel?

Maggy The way I often do before an opening night. Tense, nervous.

Ed brings a drink to her

Ed It's not knowing what the pay-off will be—that's the crunch. (*Raising his glass*) To a successful party.

Maggy Ed, are you sure this is the right way?

Ed I don't happen to be sure about a thing, honey. Let's just say it's a hunch.

Maggy The way you rely on hunches.

Ed How else can we play this? Now remember, you were attacked but you don't know how he got into your apartment.

Maggy I mustn't mention the missing key.

Ed Oh, no. You're quite sure the motive was robbery.

Maggy Suppose Peter brings the costume with him?

Ed It could prove he had nothing to do with it. Just one of those strange coincidences.

Maggy And if he doesn't bring it?

Ed We wait for his explanation.

Maggy You still think he's guilty, don't you?

Ed I could be wrong.

Maggy Turn on the electric fire, it's suddenly become chilly.

Ed (*turning on the fire*) The temperature drops when you're scared. But there's no need to be. Everything's under control.

The doorbell rings. Maggy starts, looking keyed up

Want me to get it?

Maggy No, I'd better.

Ed And remember—stick to your story.

Maggy nods and goes to answer the door

Ed takes the glasses back to the wine cabinet and remains there, listening to murmur of voices off

Maggy enters with Peter

Maggy We were wondering if your housekeeper gave you the message. Oh, I don't think you know my husband—Ed Ryde, Peter Clinton.
Ed Hi.
Peter Good evening. Maggy's often spoken about you. Aren't you the man who can sell bootlaces to people who don't wear shoes?
Ed Sure. They use 'em for neckties. What will you drink?
Peter Gin and tonic, please.

Peter moves down to the fireplace. Behind his back Ed mimes to Maggy, making the shape of a dress-box. She shakes her head

Oh, Maggy, I forgot to ask, how's your sore throat?
Maggy Much better, thanks.
Peter It hasn't developed into a cold?
Maggy It wasn't that kind of sore throat. But I'll explain about that later, when the others get here.
Peter Others? Who else is coming? If it's a party I'm afraid I won't be able to stay long. I've promised to call in at Leo's club and have a drink with him.
Maggy It's not a party. Only a get-together. Robert, Eva and George are coming.

Ed takes a drink to Peter

Peter Thanks.

Ed makes a sign to Maggy behind Peter's back

Maggy Oh, Peter, did your housekeeper mention that when we phoned this morning we inquired about—a fancy dress costume? Ed has been invited to a ball and . . .
Ed It's short notice and I don't have a thing by me to wear.
Peter You could hire a costume.
Maggy (*sitting on the settee*) Ed wanted something unusual, so we rang round and Marvells told us you'd had a costume made up by them.
Peter That's right—for the cruise.
Maggy You didn't mind their telling us, did you, Peter?
Peter Mind? Why on earth should I mind?
Ed Look, if you'd rather not lend me your costume that's okay, I'll understand. Maybe it was impertinent to ask. I just figured that as Maggy said you were an old friend—aw, let's forget it, huh?
Peter I've no objection to lending it. Did Marvells tell you what the costume was?
Maggy Yes, the Ku Klux Klan. That's really why Ed was interested—the American flavour.

Ed (*sitting in the rocker*) Not that I go around waving any flags in defence of *that* organization.

Peter Well, I'm sorry. As I said, I've no objection to lending the costume, only—it's gone.

Maggy and Ed exchange glances

Sounds crazy, I know. I kept it in a box on top of my wardrobe. Well, the box is still there but the outfit has disappeared. I asked my housekeeper about it but she said she had no idea where it could be.

Maggy Are you sure you didn't lend it to someone?

Peter I'm positive.

Maggy Now who would help themselves to a fancy dress costume?

Peter Ridiculous, isn't it? I mean, if someone wanted to borrow it, they only had to ask me.

Maggy Who knew you had it?

Peter Lots of people. I had some pictures taken on the cruise and I've shown them around. Anyway, I doubt if you'd have enjoyed the ball if you had worn that outfit. I couldn't persuade any lady passengers to dance with me. I think it scared them all off.

Ed Oh, well, it was just an idea. But it isn't important. Care for another?

Peter No, thanks. I'm all right.

Ed goes to the wine cabinet. Peter sits beside Maggy

Peter Well, Maggy, if you're quite fit now will you be at rehearsal on Monday? George phoned me. He said you'd had a talk and had decided . . .

Maggy We didn't decide anything, Peter. But when the others get here we'll discuss it, shall we?

Ed (*glancing at his watch*) They're late. (*He goes to the window and lifts the curtain to look out*)

Ed A Rolls Royce is stopping outside.

Maggy That will be Eva and Robert.

Peter One of these days Robert will get a ticket. I never dare leave *my* car in this road.

Maggy Peter, don't say anything about the missing costume to the others. It might be embarrassing.

Peter All right. But I *would* like to know who helped themselves to it.

Ed I guess the butler should have the door open to welcome the élite.

Ed goes out through the archway

Peter glances over his shoulder, then moves closer to Maggy

Peter I gather your husband has moved in. Does that mean you've come together again? I thought it was all overboard, that you were considering a divorce.

Maggy Leo doesn't approve of divorce.

Peter No, but later on, when we've got things moving and the series is established, surely then . . .

Maggy I never like to look too far ahead. It can be dangerous. (*She rises and moves up to window*)

Voices are heard off, then Ed returns with Eva and Robert

Peter rises and stands by the fireplace. Maggy goes to greet her guests

Eva Good evening, Miss Fairchild. You said it was important when you telephoned, so we've by-passed a bridge party.

Maggy It was kind of you to come at such short notice. I don't think you know my husband, Mrs Mallin.

Ed We introduced ourselves at the door. What will you drink?

Robert Eva never touches anything but vodka.

Eva It must be the influence of my Russian ancestors. White Russian, of course.

Robert (*to Ed*) Scotch for me, please.

Robert remains at the wine cabinet with Ed and helps to hand drinks round.

Maggy (*to Eva*) Do come and sit down.

Eva sits on the settee, Maggy in the basket chair

Eva Now you have a man about the house again, Miss Fairchild, I wonder you don't do something about that door downstairs. It's practically off its hinges.

Maggy It isn't really my responsibility. Anything below my flat is no-man's land.

Eva I'm afraid I couldn't live in such conditions.

Maggy One learns not to be fussy.

Peter Didn't you once tell me you discovered a tramp asleep in the passage downstairs?

Maggy Yes, poor man. He'd come in out of the rain. I brought him upstairs and gave him some breakfast.

Eva You have such a sympathetic nature, Miss Fairchild. I can just imagine your attracting vagabonds, stray cats, the lonely—and the misunderstood. (*She looks maliciously at Robert*)

Peter I'll fix that door downstairs for you some time.

Eva Peter, aren't you forgetting? Miss Fairchild has her husband back now. I'm sure Mr Ryde would hate other men doing things for his wife. Of course, while he was away it was different. In any case, Peter, shouldn't you start with your own bedroom? (*To the others*) There's a pane of glass missing from the window. He's filled it in with cardboard.

Peter (*embarrassed*) I'll get around to mending it some time. I didn't realize my guests were so observant. (*Pause*) By the way, I'm seeing Leo this evening. Can I dare tell him we'll have something ready for him to see soon?

Robert Don't make too many rash promises. If this weather continues we may not be lucky with the exterior shots.

Eva I don't know why it can't all take place in the studio.

Robert The story wouldn't amount to much if we didn't expand.

Eva Are you making excuses for a second-grade script, darling?

Maggy We all think Robert's script is excellent, Mrs Mallin.

Eva Well, naturally my opinion counts for very little.

The doorbell rings

Maggy George, I think. He did promise not to be late. And as you're all anxious to get away, we'll be as brief as possible.

Robert Are you going to make an announcement, Maggy?

Ed goes to answer the door

Peter Like walking out on us?

Eva If Miss Fairchild doesn't wish to do the series I don't think we should bring pressure to bear. There are other actresses.

Robert Eva, please! (*He sits in the rocker*)

Eva Please what, darling? Please shut up? If that's what you mean why don't you say it? If we were alone you wouldn't hesitate. It's amazing how most husbands reserve their good manners for party occasions.

Ed enters with George

George (*glancing round*) Well, hallo, am I the last?

Eva rises and goes to him. He kisses her on the cheek

Eva We wouldn't dream of starting the post mortem without you, George, darling.

George Post mortem?

Robert My wife is joking.

Eva (*leading George to the settee*) Come and sit beside me, George. In a way this is like a press conference. Miss Fairchild and her husband have called us all together because they want to make an official statement.

Ed carries a drink to George

Ed One bitter lemon. Matter of fact, Mrs Mallin, you're just about on target.

Peter moves behind the settee

Eva There, what did I tell you? We ought to have notebooks and pencils ready in the traditional reporters' style. Isn't it exciting, George? (*She hugs him close to her*) Just like a summit conference.

Robert sighs, swinging the rocker round to face front, his expression pained. Eva stares at him maliciously

What's the matter, Robert, jealous? You never like my being a success at a party, do you?

Ed If I could have your attention for a few minutes?

Ed holds out his hand to Maggy, who rises and goes to him. He puts an arm round her

You all know Maggy had to skip rehearsal yesterday morning. The reason she gave was a sore throat. True enough, she did have a sore throat—that and more. On Thursday evening she met me and we had dinner together. Around midnight she drove herself back to this apartment. (*He pauses, looking at Maggy*) Take it from there, honey.

Maggy When I came into the flat I found someone here—hiding in my wardrobe. He sprang out, caught me by the throat and tried to—strangle me!

Maggy opens her scarf to reveal the bruises. The guests exchange shocked glances. Eva rises, standing before the fireplace

Eva Would you recognize the man again? I mean, did you see his face?

Maggy No, it was dark. I'd turned off most of the lights and I was just going to bed.

Peter Why didn't you tell us this before, Maggy?

Ed Ah, that's a fair question. The only person Maggy told was me. She had her reasons.

Eva You mean you didn't call in the police?

Robert You should have done. How much was stolen?

Maggy Nothing was stolen. But I think the motive was robbery. He might not have thought I'd return so soon and he expected to take what he could find and go.

Ed As it was, Maggy disturbed him and—he tried to kill her.

Robert Thank God he didn't succeed.

Peter Didn't you even call a doctor?

Ed She did nothing and I think you all know the reason why. She didn't want the press in on this, with a lot of unfavourable publicity.

George Surely that kind of publicity wouldn't upset Leo?

Maggy It could have done. He might have suspected it was a stunt. Anyway, I was all against it.

Ed So we decided to call you together and tell you the facts.

Maggy Which are still not for publication.

Eva But if there's some housebreaker going around with murderous intent, then it's your duty . . .

Ed Maggy considered her duty was to you all. I understand this T.V. series means a lot to you.

Peter You can carry loyalty a bit too far.

Robert How did this burglar get into the flat?

Maggy I don't know. Through a window, I suppose.

George I think you should have told the police, Maggy.

Robert It isn't too late. You can still do so.

Maggy There isn't much point now.

Robert If a thing like that had happened to Eva I'd have insisted on calling the doctor and the police.

Eva (*sarcastically*) Would you, darling? How very considerate. (*She sits in the basket chair*)

Maggy My husband wanted to. We had quite a battle over it.

George So where do we go from here?

Ed May I suggest that you rest rehearsals for another week or so? Oh, I realize it's difficult—you've hired the studio space and so on—only

Maggy isn't too well. I have to fly to Scotland tonight—an important business assignment. Tomorrow Maggy is going down to Brighton to stay with an aunt of hers. She needs a rest and a change of air. When she gets back she'll be fit and ready to work again. Right now her nerves are shot to pieces and she needs time to recover.

Peter Of course we can postpone things for a while.

Maggy Are you sure? I wanted to give you an opportunity of replacing me, if you cared to.

Robert It's out of the question.

Eva You say you're going to Scotland tonight, Mr Ryde?

Ed I'm afraid I have to.

Peter Will you be all right, Maggy?

Maggy Yes. I shall go and see Ed off at the airport, and then come back and do my packing.

Ed (*looking at his watch*) I'm sorry we have to hurry you all away now. My plane is scheduled to take off at ten o'clock. So it's agreed, is it? You hold back the series for a week or so. Is that okay?

Peter There's no alternative. I'll have a word with Leo, tell him we're not quite ready.

Robert It will give me time to go over the script again and make a few adjustments. I'm not altogether satisfied.

Ed Get your coat, honey, we really must be moving.

Ed turns off the electric fire. Eva moves behind the settee next to Peter. Maggy goes towards the bedroom, turning at the door

Maggy I'm very sorry this has happened. But I think you all understand.

There are murmurs of agreement. Maggy goes into the bedroom, turns on the lights, takes a white raincoat from wardrobe, together with a white headscarf, which she puts on at mirror. Meanwhile, the conversation continues in the lounge

Eva I don't feel much like bridge after all that. I think I'll have an early night.

Robert (*rising*) Suits me.

George What's going to happen on Monday?

Peter I really haven't had time to decide yet. But I'll think of something over the week-end and give you a ring, George.

Eva If anyone is interested in my opinion I'd say this T.V. idea is bewitched. There's been nothing but trouble from the beginning. Trouble, trouble, trouble.

Robert (*going to her*) What are you talking about? We've only just started and this isn't Maggy's fault. You can't blame her for what's happened.

Eva Perhaps we should have taken out an insurance policy against misadventure.

George It will be all right, Eva.

Smiling, George goes to Eva. She fingers his coat lapels, gazing at him

Eva Yes, George, darling, but do you realize how much money it's
costing me? My father's very generous but I can't keep asking him for
an advance . . .

Ed Look, it's not my business, so maybe I shouldn't butt in, only if
Maggy's short vacation is going to unsettle your plans there is an
obvious solution.

Eva Our minds work alike, Mr Ryde. That's precisely what I was thinking.

Peter You don't mean we should find someone else?

Ed Maggy would understand.

Robert It's only a week, we can wait for her.

Eva I thought you'd say that, Robert.

Peter Why should we penalize Maggy just because she was unlucky enough
to have this rotten experience? As far as I'm concerned I don't want
anyone else in the part.

Eva You may be *compelled* to have someone else.

*Maggy turns out the bedroom lights and enters from the bedroom, wearing
her white raincoat and white headscarf*

Robert Are you driving your husband to the airport, Maggy?

Ed No, we'll get a cab.

Robert We'll give you a lift to the taxi rank.

Eva Do you want a lift, George, darling?

George Actually I want to make a phone call.

Eva Make it from here.

George No, I'll use that call-box at the end of the road.

Eva Be seeing you, then.

> *Eva and George smile at each other, then she goes out, followed by
> Robert, and then George*

Peter lingers. Ed goes into the hall to pick up his coat and hold-all

> *Peter moves to Maggy, kisses her, then goes quickly*

*Ed watches the kiss with an uplifted eyebrow. He comes down into the room,
speaking to Maggy*

Ed What was that—the kiss of Judas?

CURTAIN

SCENE 2

The same. Later that night

*The lounge and bedroom are in darkness, the curtains drawn, but the hall
light is on and the archway curtains are wide open*

*The front door opens and slams. Maggy, in raincoat and headscarf, enters
and switches on the main lights. She is followed by Ed, wearing his sheepskin
coat and carrying his hold-all*

Maggy The mud in that garden. (*She looks at her heels*) The taxi driver thought it strange, being asked to put us down in the back lane.

Ed We couldn't chance entering the front way. Your midnight visitor might be watching the house. That's if he isn't already here.

Maggy looks startled

Maggy You don't think he is, do you?

Ed I'll check. (*He goes to look in kitchen*) Okay, no-one there.

Maggy I'll make some coffee.

Maggy pulls off her headscarf and goes into the kitchen. Ed goes out to the hall and puts his hold-all in the spare room

Ed returns into the lounge, enters Maggy's bedroom, and goes to the wardrobe. He pauses a moment, then jerks open the door. Only clothes hang there, including Maggy's white négligé. He brushes them aside, searching, then closes the door and walks to the kitchen entrance

Ed All clear, Maggy.

Maggy comes from the kitchen without her raincoat and scarf

Maggy I didn't really think anyone would be here yet. Oh, Ed, your coat must be damp. I'll hang it by the boiler.

She goes to him. He removes his coat and hands it to her, then pulls her into his arms

Your coat's getting crushed.

Ed To hell with the coat!

He flings the coat on the settee and holds her to him. She does not resist

We haven't been this close for a long time. I used to dream of you back home, then I'd wake up and find you weren't there any more. At times I thought I'd go crazy, longing for you, honey.

Maggy Honestly?

Ed Sure. And how about you?

Maggy The same.

Ed Then why did you run out on me?

Maggy Oh, I don't know. The moment I boarded the plane I knew it was a mistake.

Ed You only had to catch the next jet coming back my way.

Maggy I wanted to, Ed, only I couldn't. First I had to prove I could get by on my own, establish my career again. A fine job I made of it, didn't I?

Ed Know what? We'll clear up this business, then I'm taking you home to New York.

Maggy Think it will work this time?

Ed Why not? We'll fight a little, love a lot, and I'm ready to settle for that if you are.

Maggy Totally committed?

Ed Totally committed.

He kisses her, lingeringly. Her arms go round his neck and they cling together.

As they draw apart she sighs and moves away

Maggy But I *must* work, Ed. It's terribly important to me. I can't throw aside my career and say nothing else matters, apart from being Mrs Ed Ryde.

Ed I understand, honey. Maybe I didn't at one time but I do now. Back in the States we'll find you something. There are plenty of T.V. and movie opportunities there. We might even fix you another Broadway play.

Maggy This time without George Lawrence. Poor George.

Ed When you come back with me won't it be "Poor Peter"?

Maggy I don't really think Peter's in love with me. He was just unhappy and depressed and—well, I sympathized with him.

Ed He acted mighty strange over the Klan outfit.

Maggy Ed, I've been thinking about that. You remember what Peter said —that the costume had been stolen.

Ed That was *his* story.

Maggy I think he was telling the truth. And I've just remembered something else. On Thursday when they were all here—the day the key disappeared—they were arranging another get-together for later that evening.

Ed Well?

Maggy The Mallins were on their way to a cocktail party and had asked George to go along with them. Then Peter suggested a meeting in his flat later.

Ed What are you getting at?

Maggy Don't you see? They were all there at Peter's place, and any one of them could have gone into his bedroom—and taken the costume.

Ed It's possible, I guess. But how could they conceal it from the others?

Maggy A person with murder in mind would find a way. And they all knew Peter had the Klan outfit, because of the photographs he'd had taken on the cruise.

Ed (*moving away*) Okay, so they all had access, only that doesn't mean Peter Clinton is in the clear.

Maggy (*going to him*) And another thing. You asked me yesterday who knew I was going to be out that night and I said "Only Peter". Yet if they were at his flat he could have mentioned that I was dining with you.

Ed You're quite determined to whitewash Peter Clinton.

Maggy You don't like him very much, do you?

Ed Frankly, I don't like any of that little crowd. One of them tried to murder you—and soon we'll know who it is. All we have to do now is await the killer's next move.

Maggy shivers, then picks up Ed's coat from the settee

Maggy We'll have that coffee now.

Maggie takes his coat into the kitchen

*Ed goes to the archway and closes the curtains across it. The telephone rings.
Ed whirls round, staring at it*

Maggy enters from kitchen and crosses to the telephone

Before she can lift the receiver Ed shouts at her

Ed Leave it!
Maggy But it might be . . .
Ed Sure it might be (*He goes to her.*)
Maggy Someone checking, you mean?
Ed (*nodding*) To see if you're back.
Maggy But if I'd gone to Heathrow Airport with you how could I be back yet?
Ed Exactly. But he's not taking any chances. He wants the apartment clear, so he's ringing to make sure.
Maggy Do you think he means to do things the same way as last time?
Ed Psychos usually work that way. Turn off the kitchen light.

Maggy goes to the kitchen and turns off the light there. Ed switches off the main light. Then he goes to the window and pulls back part of the curtains. A beam of blue light from the street lamp outside illuminates his face and part of the room. Maggy returns and goes to Ed

Maggy What are you doing?
Ed There's a phone booth at the end of this road.
Maggy You mean he's ringing from there. But why?

Ed places her in front of him at the window and they both stare out

Ed The nearest point to your apartment. I can just make out a dim figure in the booth. Can you see it?
Maggy Ye-es, but I can't tell who it is. The rain's too heavy, it's misting the window.

Maggy turns and moves to the telephone, staring down as it rings on relentlessly

Who hates me so much, who hates me?

The telephone stops. Maggy and Ed both stare at it, mesmerized, then Ed turns back to the window

Ed He's coming out of the call-box! And heading straight this way.
Maggy (*rushing to the window*) Who is it?
Ed Can't tell, the trees and rain blot out everything.
Maggy What do we do?
Ed Wait for him. It's my guess he'll let himself in with your key, the same as he did last time, and maybe hide in your bedroom closet.
Maggy And then?
Ed Then we catch him like a rat in a trap!

Maggy begins to shiver with apprehension. Ed grips her shoulders

Take it easy, honey. You don't have a thing to worry about.

Maggy (*emotionally, clinging to him*) If you weren't here ... Oh, Ed, darling, thank God I've got you.

Ed (*snapping his fingers*) The gun—where's the gun?

Maggy Gun?

Ed Yeah, the gun—I gave it to you. Where did you put it?

Maggy I—I can't remember.

Ed Come on, Maggy, think, think! Is it in your bedroom?

Maggy I—I don't know.

There is the sound of a key turning in the lock

Ed The front door! Someone's coming in.

As he speaks Ed grabs her hand and rushes her down into the kitchen, closing the door

Pause. Then the archway curtains twitch as someone begins to part them. The next moment they are flung wide open

Eva Mallin stands framed there. She is wearing a light-coloured raincoat with a white hood

She pauses, glancing left and right along the hall, then she comes down into the lounge, moving to the bureau. She switches on the bureau lamp and opens a drawer, searching amongst the papers. Suddenly she stops, transfixed, seeing the gun. She picks it up and, facing front, holds it in her hand, turning it over in the light from the lamp. Then she puts the gun on top of the bureau and starts to hunt for letters. She finds a bundle of them and rifles through them, facing front, her back to archway.

The light in the hall goes out

Silently a man in a shiny black raincoat and hat pulled down over his eyes, appears in the archway. He springs at the woman whose face he cannot see, his hands going round her throat from the back

Eva struggles frantically, gasping and unable to see her attacker. Her fingers grope desperately over the bureau and she finds the gun, twists her arm round and presses the muzzle into her assailant's ribs. A shot is fired

Ed and Maggy come out of the kitchen

The man collapses into the rocker, which is facing upstage. Hands pressed to his ribs, his head drops forward. Ed puts on the main lights.

Eva (*huskily*) He tried to—kill me!

Ed goes to the rocker, swivels it round and pulls off the black hat and scarf, revealing—Robert Mallin

Maggy Robert!

Eva, horrified, moves to the rocker to stare at her husband in shocked amazement. Maggy backs away. Ed puts a protective arm round her. Eva kneels beside Robert

Eva Why were you trying to kill me, Robert? For God's sake, why?

Robert (*looking at her dazedly*) I didn't know it was you, Eva, I thought it was Maggy.

Maggy and Ed exchange glances

Eva Why did you want to harm her?

Robert (*haltingly*) She was—trying to wreck George's career.

Ed What's George Lawrence to you?

Robert Ask Maggy. She knows, he told her in New York, and I—I couldn't risk her destroying my marriage . . .

Eva, realizing, straightens up, shocked

Eva Oh, God! You've never loved me, you only wanted my money.

Robert (*feebly*) Get George, I want to see George. I . . .

Robert's voice fades and he sags to the side of the chair. Ed swings it round and puts a hand over Robert's heart. Maggy hurries to the telephone.

Maggy I'll call a doctor.

Ed Too late. (*He spreads his hands eloquently*)

Eva looks at Robert, then moves away to fireplace and speaks emotionally

Eva Robert and George—and I never suspected. I thought he loved another woman. (*She looks at Maggy*) You, Maggy. I found a key in Robert's overcoat pocket and I believed you'd given it to him. So I secretly borrowed it, had a duplicate key cut, and came here tonight to find evidence for a divorce. (*She pauses, looking towards Robert*) I have my evidence now, but it no longer matters. Ring the police.

Maggy lifts the receiver, hands it to Ed and remains close to him

Ed (*to Maggy*) Did George tell you—about Robert and himself?

Maggy No. George mentioned *some* of the men in his life—but not Robert.

Ed Robert thought you knew. And he wanted to make dead sure you'd—never tell!

Ed begins to dial nine-nine-nine, as—

the CURTAIN *falls*

FURNITURE AND PROPERTY LIST

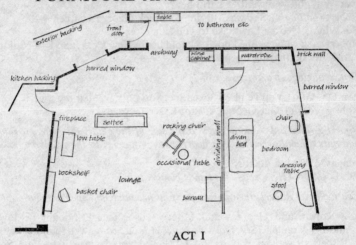

ACT I

On stage: **LOUNGE**
Settee
Basket chair
Rocking-chair
Coffee-table
Occasional table. *On it:* cigarette-box, ashtray
Bureau. *On it:* telephone, lamp, writing-pad, Biro, copy of the *Stage*,
    ashtray. *In drawers:* letters
Bookshelves. *In them:* books, ornaments, vases of flowers
Wine cabinet. *In it:* assorted drinks, including gin, Scotch, brandy,
    bitter lemon, opener, assorted glasses
On mantelpiece: cigarette-box, matches, gold lighter, ashtray, clock
By window: vacuum-cleaner
Carpet
Velvet window curtains
Archway curtain
Hearthrug

BEDROOM
Divan bed and bedding
Wardrobe. *In it:* **Maggy**'s clothes, including white négligé
Dressing-table. *On it:* cosmetics, jewel-box, ashtray, brushes, lamp,
    copy of *Spotlight*. *In drawer:* letters
Basket chair
Stool
Carpet
Window curtains

HALL:
Table. *On it:* bowl of flowers

Off stage: Door lock and knocker (for use by **Cast**)
Briefcase with T.V. script **(Robert)**
Duster **(Mrs Dacre)**
Plate of cakes **(Maggy)**
Tray with 5 cups, 5 saucers, 5 teaspoons, milk jug, sugar bowl, teapot, hot-water jug
Shopping bag **(Mrs Dacre)**
Glass of milk **(Maggy)**

Personal: **Robert:** horn-rimmed glasses, watch, Biro, lighter
Maggy: handbag with 2 keys, wallet, money and dressing, watch
Eva: Handbag
George: cigar

ACT II
SCENE 1

Off stage: Empty shopping bag **(Mrs Dacre)**
Tray with cup, saucer, spoon, sugar basin **(Mrs Dacre)**
Morning paper, letters, 2 bottles of milk **(Mrs Dacre)**
Tray with coffee-pot, cup, saucer, milk jug

Personal: **Ed:** cigarette-case, lighter, automatic, notebook, Biro, watch

SCENE 2

Strike: Glass of milk
All dirty glasses, cups, etc.
Letters, papers from coffee-table

SCENE 3

Strike: All dirty glasses

Set: Used breakfast things for 2 on coffee-table
Morning paper on settee
Copy of the *Stage*, coffee cup, notepad, Biro on floor by rocker

Off stage: Dusters **(Mrs Dacre)**

ACT III
SCENE 1

Strike: All dirty cups, dishes, etc.
Newspaper

Off stage: Bowl of ice, 2 dishes of peanuts **(Maggy)**
Leather hold-all **(Ed)**

SCENE 2

Set: Check gun in drawer of bureau
Off stage: Hold-all **(Ed)**

LIGHTING PLOT

Property fittings required: hanging lamp in HALL, wall brackets, desk lamp, dressing-table lamp, electric fire effect
A lounge and bedroom. The same scene throughout

ACT I Late afternoon

To open: All lounge practicals on. Fire out. Dusk outside window

Cue 1	**Maggy** switches on bedroom lights *Snap on bedroom practicals*	(Page 4)
Cue 2	As CURTAIN falls to denote lapse of time *Black-out except for light in hall*	(Page 16)
Cue 3	**Maggy** switches on lounge light *Snap on lounge practicals*	(Page 17)
Cue 4	**Maggy** switches on dressing-table lamp *Snap on bedroom lamp and covering Spot*	(Page 17)
Cue 5	**Maggy** switches off (a) hall and (b) lounge lights *Snap off all (a) hall and (b) lounge lighting*	(Page 17)

ACT II, SCENE 1. Morning

To open: Dim daylight in lounge. Sunlight in bedroom.
Dressing-table lamp on

Cue 6	**Mrs Dacre** draws lounge curtains *Bring up lounge lighting to full daylight*	(Page 19)
Cue 7	**Maggy** turns out bedroom lamp *Snap off lamp and covering spot*	(Page 19)
Cue 8	**Ed** switches on electric fire *Bring up electric fire effect*	(Page 22)

ACT II, SCENE 2. Night

To open: All practicals on. Fire out

No cues

ACT II, SCENE 3. Morning
To open: General effect of daylight. Fire out
No cues

ACT III, SCENE 1. Evening

To open: Lounge and hall practicals on. Bedroom in darkness.
Fire lit

Cue 9	**Ed** turns on the fire	(Page 39)
	Bring up electric fire effect	
Cue 10	**Ed** turns out electric fire	(Page 45)
	Fade fire	
Cue 11	**Maggy** switches on bedroom lights	(Page 45)
	Snap on bedroom practicals	
Cue 12	**Maggy** switches off bedroom lights	(Page 46)
	Snap off bedroom practicals	

ACT III, SCENE 2.   Night

To open: Hall light only on

Cue 13	**Maggy** switches on lounge lights	(Page 46)
	Snap on lounge wall brackets	
Cue 14	**Maggy** goes into kitchen	(Page 49)
	Snap off kitchen strip	
Cue 15	**Ed** switches off main lights	(Page 49)
	Snap off all practicals	
Cue 16	**Ed** draws lounge curtains	(Page 49)
	Bring up beam of light in lounge from street lamp	
Cue 17	**Eva** switches on bureau lamp	(Page 50)
	Snap on lamp and covering spot	
Cue 18	**Eva** rifles through letters	(Page 50)
	Snap off hall lamp	
Cue 19	**Ed** switches on main lounge lights	(Page 50)
	Snap on lounge wall brackets	

EFFECTS PLOT

ACT I

ACT II
Scene 1

Scene 2

Scene 3

ACT III
Scene 1

SCENE 2

Cue 14	**Ed** draws archway curtains	(Page 49)
	Telephone rings—continue until Cue 15	
Cue 15	**Maggy:** "...Who hates me?"	(Page 49)
	Telephone stops ringing	

MADE AND PRINTED IN GREAT BRITAIN BY
LATIMER TREND & COMPANY LTD PLYMOUTH
MADE IN ENGLAND